Secrets of Screen Acting

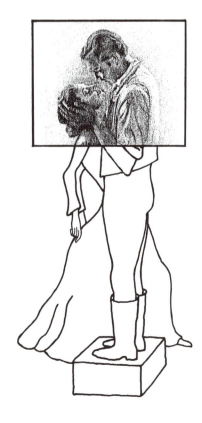

Secrets of Screen Acting

by Patrick Tucker

Illustrations by John Stamp

A Theatre Arts Book
Routledge • New York and London

Published in 1994 by

Routledge
29 West 35th Street
New York, NY 10001

Published in Great Britain by

Routledge
11 New Fetter Lane
London EC4P 4EE

Library of Congress Cataloging-in-Publication Data

Tucker, Patrick.
    Secrets of screen acting / by Patrick Tucker.
        p.   cm. — (A Theatre Arts book)
    Includes bibliographical references and index.
    ISBN 0-87830-041-4 : ISBN 0-87830-042-2 :
    1. Motion picture acting—Vocational guidance.   2. Acting for television—Vocational guidance.   I. Title.   II. Series.
PN1995.9.A26T8   1993
791.43'028'023—dc20   93-28890
                                                                             CIP

For my partner Christine

TABLE OF CONTENTS

INTRODUCTION

Acting on screen is more like real life.	**Not true.**
When acting for television, just make everything smaller.	**Not true either.**
For film, it is all in the eyes.	**If only it were that simple.**
Do less with your face on screen.	**If anything, the opposite is true.**
As an actor, I do exactly the same on screen as I do on stage.	**Oh no you don't.**

Inside this book you will find the answers to the problems posed here—and a whole lot more.

This book is written to answer that simple but profound question: what do you actually **do** that's different when acting or presenting on screen, either in film or television? It is mainly for actors (and teachers of acting), but it also has special chapters for announcers and interviewees and for directors.

The differences between film, television and stage acting are carefully defined, as are all aspects of being part of the screen business. It tells you what you **do** when performing in one medium or the other. It is invaluable for anyone who has anything at all to do with the screen, large or small.

If you are interested in what actually happens to actors when they get on the screen, then this book will tell you things you have never come across before.

I shall use the term "screen" when I believe the point raised applies both to the large (movie) and the small (television) screen. Points that are particular to only one medium will be identified as such.

It is impossible to be neutral when I am talking to you, and equally impossible to find a general term to cover both the sexes. I shall address you alternatively by chapter as "she" and "he." This choice is random, and there will be no connection between choice of gender for a chapter and the topic covered in it. The term "actor," of course, covers both female and male performers.

Some while back I gave a presentation at the American Theater Association (now alas no more) entitled "Screen Acting **Should** Be Taught; It **Can** Be Taught; Here's **How.**" I had a very large and enthusiastic response but was completely unable to answer the question, "which book did you get this from?" and equally unable to give a good answer to "but where can we learn more about all this?"

This book is a belated response to those requests.

ACKNOWLEDGMENTS

This book started life with a letter: "Sometimes the way to get books to happen is to put contracts in the post. So I'm doing just that," and so without Bill Germano's spur, and the support from the team at Routledge, this book would not have started or finished.

I started to write it when I was working on television dramas in Vordingborg, Denmark; Dublin, Ireland; and Liverpool, England; and finished in London and New York; so directly and indirectly I owe thanks to TV2 Øst's *Landsbyen*, Radio Telefís Éireann's *Fair City*, and Mersey Television's *Brookside*.

I started my television acting classes at the Drama Studio London, the specialist U.K. One Year Graduate Acting Programme, in 1975 and have continued them there and at other drama schools in the U.K. and in the United States. The main thanks and acknowledgments go to the Executive Director of the DSL, Peter Layton, who encouraged me to present and develop a brand new acting class; and to Tim Oman, then Doug Moston, and now John Basil and the American Globe Theatre (and the Margots), who have all helped to bring my workshops to New York so successfully.

I would also like to thank Trevor Owens for the photograph of me on the set of *Brookside*; Dave Hutchman for his thoughts on "then" and "now"; and to Christine who, amongst many other burdens, had to sit through the *Rambo* films doing the word count.

Chapter One

Screen versus Stage

Clint
Eastwood
and
Lee Marvin

SCREEN VERSUS STAGE

We are all stage actors

Oh yes we are. You may not actually have walked the boards to perform (at least not since school), but every time we want to get our way by putting on an "act," we are "acting," and because it is for someone at a reasonable distance away from us—a "real" distance—it is stage acting.

The child wanting her own way who cries real tears, which are miraculously cleared when she gets it, is giving a particularly convincing "performance."

The stern authoritarian voice you put on when complaining about bad service in a shop is another.

The fawning words and actions we all go through when pulled over for speeding, and the subsequent fake smiles, comprise yet another performance aimed at a particular audience.

These are moments when we are using our words and bodies to convince someone of some emotion or thought that may not, in fact, be the literal truth of what we are feeling but is the emotion we want the other person to **believe** we are experiencing. This is what stage actors do, too.

Very few of us—especially, funnily enough, screen directors—have experience in acting for the screen or know what the difference would be between this and the acting mentioned above.

When I ask people of no experience, limited experience or who are very experienced indeed what the difference is between "screen" performing and "stage" performing, I get surprisingly uniform answers.

From professional actors and students both in the United States and the United Kingdom, here is a selection of the answers I have heard to the following question:

What difference would you make, if any, between acting on screen compared with acting on stage?

Do less.

Make it more real.

Make it more intimate.

Tone it all down.

Make it more internal.

Scale down your performance.

Be more still.

Make fewer facial expressions.

Be smaller.

Be more natural.

These are the most common reactions—**and they are all wrong!**

Usually in a list of ten items I am given by a class or group, seven or eight will be variations from this wrong list. One Method drama school in England even graduated its students recently with the declaration that they were probably better prepared for television than the theater, since they had been trained to be minutely realistic; this from a course where over the three years they never once appeared on a screen or ever got down to analyzing what screen acting might be.

In the old days young stage actors learned from older, experienced professionals, by watching and by acting with them. The young apprentices would play small roles, and stand in the wings watching the master actors at work, hoping one day to be able to copy them and, in their turn, to be copied.

How My Classes *Think* Screen Acting Differs from Stage Acting

Do less.

Make it more real.

Make it more intimate.

Tone it all down.

Make it more internal.

Scale down your performance.

Be more still.

Make fewer facial expressions.

Be smaller.

Be more natural.

How many professional stage productions have **you** seen in your lifetime—that is, productions where you paid to watch and the actors were paid to perform?

Twenty? Fifty? One hundred? Let's be generous, and make it three hundred. (That **was** generous, wasn't it?)

So how many **hours** of professional stage acting have you watched?

Nine hundred? Again, let's be generous, and make it an even thousand—and for most of you, you **know** that you have not experienced that many hours of professional stage acting.

And how many hours of professional **screen** acting have you seen? How many?

Current estimates indicate that by the time you have left your teen years, you have watched between ten thousand and twenty thousand hours of screen stuff.

And yet, and yet, most people have no idea what screen performing involves, and always relate their idea of it to **stage** versions of acting.

Strange, isn't it?

To start at the beginning

On screen, you can be seen in anything from a full-length shot of your whole body to a big close-up of your face, depending on the size of shot. I must be able to talk to you about these different sizes, but unfortunately there is no worldwide acceptance of what a size of shot **means**, and there are even variations within countries. My definitions are, I believe, the most widely used, but there is considerable confusion as to what "medium close-up" means, for example, and it is always necessary to describe your shots to establish a common vocabulary. What follows are the descriptions that I shall be using for the rest of the book, with noted variations.

Onto the TV screen comes a picture of a woman. Her head is at the top of the screen, her toes at the bottom. This is called a Long Shot (LS).

Most people watch a television screen that is about twenty to twenty-two inches wide, and about eight to ten feet away from them. Try now, if you can, watching a blank screen ten feet away and picturing this image on it: the full-length shot of a woman.

Now, how far away would you have to be in a theater to see an actor this size? Yes, it is about sixty-five feet—or the back row of a large theater.

And how do actors convey thought, action and mood to an audience this far away? Yes, through whole body motions and attitudes as well as loud voices, for it is very difficult to see detailed expressions on their faces.

Next shot: the Mid-Shot (MS). Here the woman still has her head at the top of the screen, but now the image is larger, and we can only see down to her waist. This is the usual size of shot when there are two or three people on the screen together.

And where in the theater would you expect to see people **this** size? Yes, about half way back in the orchestra *(U.S.)*, or stalls *(U.K.)*. Actors here can use some of their facial expressions, but they still have to use their bodies.

Next: the Medium Close-Up (MCU). This is where you see the actor's head and shoulders, with the bottom of the frame cutting across the actor at chest level. Where would you be in the theater now?

The odds are you have chosen the front row, for this size shot is the equivalent to a distance of about ten feet—yes, the medium close-up is the size a person would be **if they were standing where your television set is.** In other words, there is a relationship with real life for this size, and it is no coincidence that this is the most popular size of shot in television drama.

(I seem to have concentrated on television for this section. The size of shots in films—films as shown in movie houses—are a little different, with the images tending to be shot a bit looser than television. In the classic John Ford film *Stagecoach* there is barely a shot closer than a medium-shot. Mind you, since most films now gain essential revenue by being shown on television in their second run or being released very soon on video, the sizes of images in the movies are getting larger, and correspond more to the televisual style of shooting.)

And how does an actor communicate when the audience is only ten feet away? Well, with subtlety, expressions, small facial tics and so on, just as they would in a "real" situation.

Adjust Scale of Performance to Size of Shot	
Long Shot	Large, melodramatic style of acting
Mid Shot	"Intimate" theater style
Medium Close-Up	Reality
Extreme Close-Up	Think it

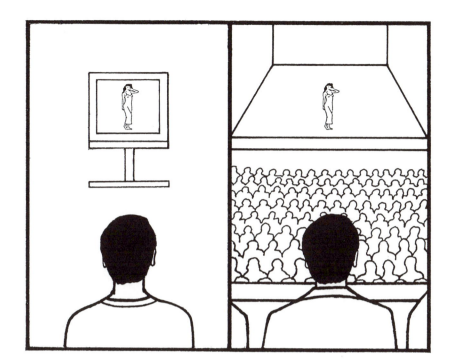

Balcony
view

Mid-
orchestra
view

8

Front
orchestra
view

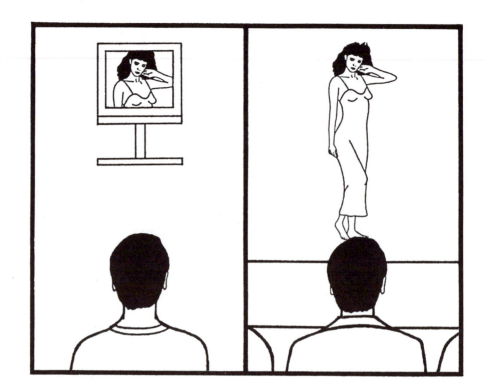

Intimate
view

The story does not end here, for there is another size of shot to talk about, where the face entirely fills the screen, from the eyebrows to the chin: Extreme Close-Up (ECU), known as Big Close-Up (BCU) in the U.K. And where would you be in a theater to get **this** view of an actor?

You would probably have to climb into bed with an actor to get your face close enough to "see" her this size, and by the time you were that close, your eyes would be out of focus anyway—so you **never** see a real person in the same way as this gigantic close-up. But it doesn't stop us from using it! It is, if you like, an unreal size of shot, and might correspond to seeing what someone is **thinking** rather than presenting.

Actors on tour with a production that is going to play in different theaters learn to adapt their performances according to whether they are playing in a large, medium or intimate theater. They alter their performances from venue to venue, from week to week.

Since screen acting involves many different shot sizes, I would state that the screen actor must be prepared to adapt her performance from shot to shot.

In other words, you must change your performance **according to the size of shot.**

Long shot:	**Large, melodramatic style of acting**
Medium shot:	**"Intimate" theater style**
Medium Close-Up:	**Reality**
Extreme Close-Up:	**Think it**

Simple now, don't you think?

On page 11 are the shot sizes of an actor, one strip where she keeps doing the same thing with the camera getting tighter and the other where she adapts what she is doing to the size of shot. (No guessing which I prefer. Which do you?)

Watching the Stage versus Watching the Screen

You see, when members of an audience are watching a stage play, they have choices of where to look. They can look at the speaker, or the listener or the servant in the corner. They can study the scenery, the lighting or even the head of the person sitting in front of them if the play is too boring.

As far as the screen is concerned, there is nothing else to look at except the moment presented by the production team. So it **has** to have greater significance, since the audience has to get **everything** from this one picture, rather than having a whole range of images to choose from.

There is another fundamental difference between stage and screen, especially the television screen. In the theater we see the actor by reflected light, while on the screen the image is itself transmitting light. This makes a television image very compelling. (And fatal for those trendy stage directors who like to imitate life by putting a television set on stage and then have it showing something. Recently I watched a production in London which did this, and the audience happily watched the previous night's news and commercials on the television screen while the poor stage actors tried unsuccessfully to compete.)

We are now so used to watching the screen, that when a lecturer I know used a TV screen to show herself to the back of a remote hall, she found that the audience near her preferred to watch her on the screen rather than in the flesh. What was more upsetting was that they still watched the screen when the image went wrong, and only "snow" was showing!

From real life to stage to screen

Imagine two people talking to each other in real life. What changes would they make in the way they are doing this if the moment were to be presented on a stage? Maybe they would talk a little louder, maybe they would turn their shoulders out a little to present more of their faces to the audience but, on the whole, there would be a very close similarity between the "real life" version and the "stage" version.

And if this moment were to be shown on the screen? Here the changes could be dramatic, with one actor standing **very** close to the other, or standing behind her talking into her hair. If both actors are to be in the same shot there has to be a radical departure from what they would do in "real" life in order to be able to put them on screen giving the **impression** of real life. This is called cheating. Look again at the pictures at the beginning of

Differences between Screen and Stage

Screen	Stage
• audience told where to look	• audience chooses where to look
• very different from "real life"	• close to "real life"
• steady state for character	• character changes and grows
• change acting style from shot to shot	• change acting style from theater to theater

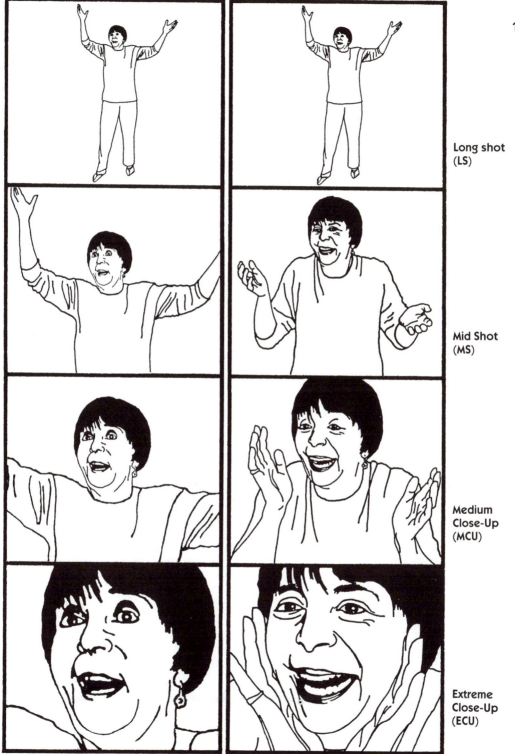

Long shot
(LS)

Mid Shot
(MS)

Medium
Close-Up
(MCU)

Extreme
Close-Up
(ECU)

this chapter. The one of Clint Eastwood and Lee Marvin very close together is exactly as they were in a particular moment of the movie *Paint Your Wagon*. The second picture is how they might be in "real life," for two such masculine men would hardly be rubbing up against each other as closely as in the film version.

If this seems a little strange, stop reading this right now and turn on the television to watch a film or television drama **with the sound off** (so you don't get distracted by the story line). Watch how the actors **really** stand in relationship to each other; see for yourself what the positions are; start noticing (for the first time?) all the **cheating** that goes on to make it all **appear** real.

There is a lot more of why this cheating is necessary in Chapter Three—the Frame and Chapter Four—the Camera.

Dramatic Structure

The structure of dramas on screen, especially television, is often very different from that of stage dramas, especially when dealing with soap operas or shows with regular characters. Apart from the results of typecasting (where a performance is known before it is seen—see Chapter Seven—Typecasting), there is also the fact that the normal dramatic form of change and growth cannot be used, for a character has to be more or less the same from episode to episode, from year to year. That is, of course, why people watch serial dramas, to lend some stability to a challenging world. Viewers **like** to know that Agent 007 will, whatever the trauma, survive at the end or that this particular character will always win the court case, and that one will always lose.

This leads to my Theory of Suffering: regular television dramas must present characters suffering so that the audience can feel that at least someone they know is having a worse time than themselves. In real life we do not know how events will turn out, whether we will cope well with the unknowns of life, but we **can** tune in and find that J.R. is still the same sly dog we remembered all those episodes ago; Inspector Morse will always solve the murder case; and Roseanne will live and fight on to face another emotional crisis on our behalf.

At a conference on soap dramas in Germany a couple of years ago, I presented the thought that American soap operas tend to show rich people suffering while in the United Kingdom they tend to show poor people suffering. I then watched the latest German offering in this form and came to the conclusion that it had middle-class people going through the various traumas on behalf of their audience.

So for the actor—learn how to present the maximum suffering and anguish, and just wait for the jobs to roll in! (I think you can detect some tongue in cheek around here, although John Barrymore, when asked why he chose to portray a smaller part to a larger one in a movie, declared he always went for the character who did the most suffering!)

Actors on stage versus on screen

A lot of actors talk a lot of sense about the differences between the two media (see Richard A. Blum's useful book *Working Actors*), but when asked about acting they will often tell the questioner what they think people want to hear, rather than what they know.

Because actors chosen to act in the movies come from a pool of thousands, those chosen tend to be those who tend to act "naturally" for the screen, whether they know it or not. Some of the reasons they give, then, for their expertise are not always the actual ones.

I was working with a wonderful elderly actor in New York, who claimed that there was no difference at all between her work on stage and on screen. She had trained in Stanislavski techniques, and they worked just as well for screen as stage, she declared. As we continued to work, she would acknowledge that the things I was talking of were, in fact, also what she did. By the end of the workshop I had a whole long list of things that she now admitted she did differently on screen than on stage. This is not to criticize her (in fact, I come across this very often), but it shows that what she **said** she did with her acting was not what she actually **did**, and she was very skillful and deservedly successful. Many actors will talk of what they think they are expected to say, rather than talk about the reality of working professionally on the screen. (The leading questions asked of them—"You always think the thoughts of the character you are playing, don't you?"—force them into these positions.)

Some experienced actors will make statements along the lines of, "It has taken me all these years to learn to do nothing on screen—I just think it." Young actors, reading this, joyfully rush in to do the same and find to their horror that their performances don't exist, they are invisible.

There are two other interesting aspects of this phenomenon. First, as an actor gets more experienced in screen work, she **automatically** does those things I am talking about without realizing it, just as when you start to drive a car it seems impossible to talk and shift gears at the same time, but some while later you can chat along with the best of us. The other reason is even more revealing: a star brings onto the screen not only her face and personality but also our memory of her past successful performances. **This** colors our observations of what she does. When Sylvester Stallone gives a small glance, we (who know his past performances of violence and action) will read menace into it, whereas with an unknown actor giving exactly the same glance, we will have gathered—nothing. When Spencer Tracy gives an enigmatic look, we (remembering his past performances of honorable characters) read into it a whole lot of subtlety that, if you or I were to be as enigmatic, would be read as—enigmatic. A drinking problem, sexual hang-up or particular neurosis in our stars (all lovingly revealed by the mass media) adds to our appreciation of a performance, and the producers include this background into their casting choices. One has only now to see a picture of Woody Allen, for example, and a whole world of assumptions kick in without him having to act a thing.

King Vidor writes of acting on screen, "I want everything to look real, but not necessarily be real." Elia Kazan, the great Method director, writes that "the art of motion pictures is one of photographing looks, not photographing dialogue."

Videotaping theater performances

All attempts to videotape live theater performances (and so get cheap television!) have failed, offering further proof of the great difference between acting for the stage and for the screen.

Unless the company is prepared to invest millions in a production—as with Trevor Nunn's stage production of *Nicholas Nickleby* where they did a **film version** of the stage presentation that took six weeks to rehearse and put in the can—attempts to bring video cameras into a theater and get something worthwhile cannot work. The style and approach of the actors are hopelessly compromised: Should they project for the live audience or for the camera? Should they position themselves for the live audience out front or for the cameras that will inevitably be there on either side of them, trying to "get onto their eyelines"?

The end result is usually poor television—and poor theater. Oh, for archival purposes it can be useful to stick a camera at the back of an auditorium and film the result, but it is still only a record of what happened that day and not a true account of the theatrical experience.

The *Nicholas Nickleby* production worked on screen because all the performers were giving **film** performances, while giving the appearance of doing stage ones. That is also why it took so long to film.

The British actor Ian Richardson was in New York and saw that they were going to show a video recording of the famous production of *Marat/Sade* that he had starred in some ten years before. He sat at the back of the auditorium to see it; he was not so much shocked that the audience thought it bad and laughable, but that he found it that way, too. Theater exists in the eyes of its audience, and to take it out of its context (like Laurence Olivier's *Othello*—please, please don't see it on tape; you will see a dreadful screen performance that nowhere suggests the genius and brilliance of that performance in the theater) is to take away something irreplaceable. That production Ian Richardson appeared in **was** brilliant—at the time it was seen in the theater by the audience, who correctly gave it a standing ovation each night.

So don't laugh at old films of the famous nineteenth-century actress Sarah Bernhardt; they do not show the real theatricality. The two media are not compatible and need very different approaches to make each shine at its best.

I went back to my old college some while ago to give a two-day seminar on screen acting. On the second day, some of the participants, students training to be professional actors, did not turn up. The reason given was that they had decided they were only going to do theater in their careers. (It also had a lot to do with me telling them their types—see the chapter on Typecasting—and they did not like what they heard.) Well, how nice to be so sure about such an uncertain profession, and such an uncertain future!

Continuous versus disjointed acting

I have left until last in this chapter what most people put first—that on the stage the actor starts at the beginning and goes to the end, building and changing in one long, continuous event, while for the screen the actor is often asked to act scenes wildly out of context and out of time order.

I put it last because, frankly, although it is a major difference, I don't find it changes what the actor has to do all that much. I know perfectly well that it might mean that the screen actor has to perform her last scene before getting to the first one, but actors do that sort of jumping around in stage rehearsals, and although it is a correct **observation** that this is what happens for the screen, I do not see it has any great **effect** on what actors do. After all, they are required to act a scene, so they act it, with as much background and detail as they can.

What the actor **does** then is substantially the same as what she does for any other sort of acting as far as preparation and performing is concerned. No, the differences between stage and screen acting are the more significant ones outlined earlier in this chapter and expanded in the rest of the book.

Chapter Two

Film versus Television

Arnold
Schwarzenegger

FILM VERSUS TELEVISION

What is the difference between film and television? What is the difference between the big screen and the small screen? As one underemployed film editor asked me, "Which do **you** prefer working with, silver or rust?" They say this because the original chemical used in film stock was silver iodide that went black when exposed to light, and the first video recordings were made on tape coated with iron oxide, or rust.

I know, of course, that many productions made on film are intended to be shown on the small screen of television, and that practically no productions made on video for the small screen are ever shown on the big screen of a movie house. To prevent confusion, in this section when I say "film," I mean a production that is primarily intended to be shown on a large screen in a public place; I will use "television" to include those productions, recorded either on film stock (silver) or videotape (rust), that are intended to be shown on the small screen in a private place.

The silver and rust comment shows the antagonism often felt toward video, with film somehow thought of as the more "pure" medium. Certainly, film can do a lot that video cannot, and it is helpful (and useful for the actor) to know why.

The recording media

(Film stock for film or television; videotape only for television.)

A picture that is recorded on celluloid can accept a range of light greater than a picture recorded on videotape. One of the reasons for this is that the "contrast ratio" of a video camera insists that the light level remain within a certain range. It has to, for, unlike film where to be whiter than white simply means the picture gets "burnt out" making quite a nice effect, the television screen can only show the brightest thing it sees as its whitest bit. If the **contrast** between the brightest bit (a very sunny wall for example) and the face of the actor is very great, then the television screen will show the wall as a wall, and the actor's face will appear black. In fact, to make the actor's face appear at all normal, it will have to be lit so that the **contrast** between the brightness of the face and the brightness of the wall is less, and is in the television's acceptable range.

This **does** affect the actors, for if they appear in a video in front of a window, and the sun does or does not come out, there may be a delay while the crew put up or take down gels or scrim in the window, fade up or down extra lights, in order to change the light level, correct the contrast and so allow the actor's face to be seen. To understand this, and therefore help, or at least not get upset by the inevitable delays while the problem is sorted out, is the actor's contribution to the process. In film, because the brightest bit can be allowed to burn out, different lighting techniques are used that are not as restrictive as those for video.

The actual picture as recorded on film (blobs of chemicals changing color according to the light falling on them) or on videotape (an electron beam detecting whether or not an electron has been knocked out of orbit on an electrostatically charged screen) leads to different audience response to the two media. Observers tend to believe that a film image corresponds more to what we **think** we see, whereas an electronic image is more "truthful"—and therefore **less** like what we think we see.

To explain. The actual "degree of resolution"—the amount of detail that can be distinguished—is less for video than for film. The limitations on video are the number of lines used (525 in the US, 625 in the UK), and the number of dots on the television set's tube that can be excited by the electron beam. The limitation on film is the density of the chemicals that change color as light falls upon them—and we now have very fine grained films indeed. So film can record more accurately the detail of leaves on a tree than video can. But what happens when the leaves move?

A moving object on film will—because it only samples once every 25th of a second—be a series of frozen moments in time, shown rapidly one after another, without the in between bits being recorded at all; film if you like always shows "then". A moving object recorded on video will, because the video picture is continuously scanned from top to bottom, always be showing some part of the picture that is actually happening at that moment; it always shows "now". You can test this by viewing old movies or old videos—the videos might be technically inferior, but they always seem somehow more immediate. Another factor that makes video appear different is that because the screen is scanned from top to bottom every $1/60$ of a second ($1/50$ in the UK), there will be the peculiarity that the top of something (your head) will very fractionally move before the bottom (your feet).

Film tends to be shot with only one camera at a time—setups for a big explosion or car crash are the obvious exceptions—so each shot is lined up and shot, and then the crew and cast move on to the next one.

Video is often shot in a multicamera studio, that is, where there are many cameras (I have had up to six in one studio); the actors do their pieces, and the cutter *(U.S.)* or vision mixer *(U.K.)* cuts between the cameras to record what is essentially an already-edited result. This naturally leads to a very different approach to acting than just working for one camera and one shot at a time.

There is a trend now, especially in low-cost dramas, to make them with **single camera video**, that is, to use one video camera to record the images and so make the project in a "filmic" way. Contrary to many people's imaginings (including many in the profession itself), it is **not** necessarily better to have many cameras, nor is it slower to shoot with a single camera. On *Brookside,* the soap drama I have done most work on in the U.K., the director gets an average of 12½ minutes of broadcastable drama per day out of its single camera video system, so in six shooting days enough is shot for three 25-minute episodes. Excellent work can be done, still using tracks and jib arms, but everyone, actors included, has to be very accurate, talented and fast, for they are attempting to do things in a filmic way without the budget or time to do so. I feel this is going to be an increasing trend in the future, as budgets contract and demand for low budget drama increases.

How many minutes a day?

If you were to work on a major movie, it is possible that the producers would expect the cast and crew to put between one and two minutes a day of finished material into the can. If it were a drama made on film but destined for the television screen, then they would perhaps expect to finish six minutes a day. If it is single camera video, making a regular soap opera on location, then they can expect up to fifteen minutes a day. So you can see that there must inevitably be a different level of expectation for each style of shooting and a different standard to be achieved. Although the technicians may be rushed, and the crew cannot do take after take to achieve perfection, there will still be the expectation that the acting should be perfect, whether you have had to prepare one or fifteen minutes of dialogue.

For a multicamera drama, of course, you can be expected to deliver a great deal more each shooting day—anything up to sixty minutes of finished drama at one studio, although the lines would normally be split between quite a number of regular performers.

As you can see, the television actor is expected to digest and perfect a great deal more material than the pure film actor—**and** he gets paid less. No wonder you all want to end up as one of Hollywood's finest!

Editing

All around the world students of film study hard and spend months inside a cutting room carefully assembling their student projects, while in the Big Bad World of the profession you might have one day to edit a 30-minute drama made on video or only a few weeks to edit a drama shot on film. All those experiments that you wanted to try out—the alternative order of shots, the interesting montage of shots that would tell the story in pictures—well, in the real world you often just do not have the **time** to experiment. You have to know what you want before you shoot it, and then go out and do it. See Chapter Eleven—Directing Actors for the Screen for more information about what difference this editing time has on the way directors work with actors.

Watching the screen

If we all decided to go see a film today, that is the first point: we have to **decide** to go, and we have to choose where to go.

We travel to **their** place, pay money to get in and, hopefully, find an auditorium that has some elements of luxury about it. Even if the red plush curtains have disappeared, we will still have attendants and people selling us goodies.

We sit in a large room with quite a few other people, and, to help us concentrate on the film, the lights are dimmed while the movie is playing.

When the film starts, we gaze up at these **large** creatures who fill our fields of vision. If, unfortunately, people near us talk or rustle paper, some of us have been known to hiss "Shhh!" If, even more unfortunately, we do not like the movie, well, we have paid to get in, so often we stay to the bitter end, hoping it will get better or, in any event, will give us our money's worth.

When it is over we return to our own homes. Then we can recommend (or not) that our friends repeat our experience, for the film will be showing again.

For television, all is different.

For a start, it is easy to watch television without really **deciding** to do so—it just happens to be on so often.

When we watch the screen, the lights are not dimmed, and the screen is surrounded by elements of **our** lives: our potted plant, our books and papers, our false teeth in a glass. Look again at the picture of Arnold Schwarzeneger at the beginning of this chapter. Does it seem familiar?

If anyone moves in the room while we are watching TV, our eyes flick to that person. We often look away from the screen—to talk, to eat, to flirt—why, we even leave the room for a short while in the middle of a program without feeling we are missing much.

We talk while the TV set is on, since the **small** creatures have been "invited" into our homes. What's more, if any of them upsets or annoys us at any time—**zap!** We can get rid of them at the touch of a button. And if the program is recorded on video, we can stop to rewind and look at any bit we like (or dislike) again, pick up any mistakes, freeze-frame over the shot of the murderer's feet to see exactly whose shoes they are. In short, the performers work entirely at **our** convenience. (I recently happened to be watching a video of a World War II German propaganda film and was able to freeze-frame Hitler—with sweaty arm pits! **That** image would have been snipped out if the filmmakers knew that one day we could push a "pause" button.)

Our relationship to the television screen is just so **different** from our relationship to the movie screen.

Mind you, television people often do not show a theatrical film the way it was made by its original talents but edit the film for so-called good reasons. They crop the picture to fit the television screen (and sometimes artificially pan left or right to get people's heads in or artificially cut from one head to another whereas the original had two people on a wide screen talking to each other); they dub different words over so-called profanity; they have even been known to speed up a film by a small amount (dropping the sound frequency so that the actors' voices do not sound squeaky) giving them more time to show commercials! And the sound quality from a television set, even the latest models, has a long way to go to match the sound you can get in a movie house.

Pictures versus words

In the movies, the filmmakers can often tell a story purely by pictures—a whole series of pictures that by their composition, juxtapositions and so on give you the atmosphere, mood and feeling of what is going on. Often for a major action movie, the amount of lines spoken is frighteningly small. (**How** few lines for **how** many bucks did Sylvester Stallone say in *Rambo III*? Actually it was 592 words, well down from his appearance in *First Blood* and a grand total of 861.)

On television, no program maker would dare leave you alone with pictures for too long, for you look away frequently and, by missing one of the pictures or images, you would no longer be able to follow the story. On television, then, the story will more often than not be **on the sound track**. This means that even if the viewer is looking away (or out of the room) he will be able to follow the story and follow the action. **That** is why characters talk nonstop in soap operas—they have no choice. They must entertain and inform even when the viewer is in the middle of going to the bathroom, eating a meal or—and here you can fill in your **own** favorite TV-watching activity.

Single camera versus multicamera

Suppose there is a short scene to be shot of a group of you listening to someone giving a lecture, and one of you turns to the other and says, "This is boring!" and the other replies "Shhh." How shall I put this on screen?

Let us pretend that you are the one saying the line, and I am the director. If I am doing it with a single camera (either film **or** video) then I would place you in a real room (no need for a studio and its expensive sets), I would set up the camera to do a group shot (over the lecturer's shoulder toward the group, for instance), and I would set the lights so the room and the students looked just right. I would then record the whole scene—I would get my master shot.

The crew would then move the camera and **move the lights**, so the camera was pointing at and giving me a close-up of the "This is boring!" speaker— you. Furniture would have to be moved to make space for the camera and lights, and maybe a reflector board would be brought in to remove the bags from under your eyes—oh, all the activity involved to get a shot that looks just right. I would have the lights adjusted so that there is only one light (your key light) reflected, to give that wonderful single point of intensity in the middle of your eyes. (You should, by the way, aim to get the same effect when your photograph is taken. There is no need for it not to be there. Several lights in your eyes can make you look shifty, and so can the white dot [the reflected light] if it is to one side of your eye.)

Then I would record your moment. My happy boom operator would be able to

Differences between Film and Television

Film	Television
• made with silver	• made with rust
• usually uses single camera	• often uses multicamera
• uses cheap film editing	• uses expensive video editing
• usually on the big screen	• always on the small screen
• public viewing	• private viewing
• viewed in dark	• viewed in light
• storyline often told in pictures	• storyline always told in words

get the microphone in just so, to record nice, intimate sound. Maybe I don't like the way you say the line, maybe you don't; in all I could easily do a number of takes of the line "This is boring!" with a little acting note attached to each, and **you don't know which one I am going to use**.

I would then get the crew to move the camera to your friend, repeat all the business of moving lights and getting a perfect shot before recording the replied "Shhh." Again, I may ask for several takes of the "Shhh" to get various versions for me to play with in editing. (The "This is boring!" person need not, of course, be there for this. I could just get the "Shhh" person to say the line to a mark.)

I take the three **setups** I have recorded either to the film or video editing room, where I cut them together. As you can see, I am not cutting together events that took place in real time, I am creating the moment out of a variety of "This is boring!"s and "Shhh"s—and, particularly with film, I can spend quite a bit of time playing around until the effect is right.

And how would I record this moment in a multicamera setup? Well, for a start, I would not bring all my cameras and associated crew to a small room; I would have them build a replica of part of the room in a studio. I would rehearse with the group of students in real time, getting what I wanted **from the actual performance**. I would place three cameras: one behind the lecturer looking over his shoulder towards the students, one looking at the face of the "This is boring!" speaker and another camera tucked away for the face of the "Shhh" person.

Unfortunately, I cannot put the cameras in the correct places to get properly balanced shots. Although with the individual camera setups I could put the camera where I wanted, now I can only put a camera where it will not be seen by the others, even if this means that the shot is not quite what I want. The pictures are then a compromise of what I would like, not as well composed or balanced as the single camera setup. Noticeably, the lighting for the three cameras is inferior to the lighting I got for the individual camera. It is not just because I cannot put in the reflector board to remove the bags under your eyes because it would be seen by another of the cameras. The lighting will be compromised, and let me explain why.

Very approximately, to light an actor's face you need a key light (to give the glow and dot in the center of the eye), a back light (to define the edge of the head against the background) and the fill light (to, well, to fill in the shadows). With a single camera setup, it is possible to get all these lights in the correct places and light the face well. With a three (or more) camera setup it is impossible, since with all those lights (each camera needing a key, back and fill), there will be many little white dots in the centers of the eyes. A light that is a correct key for one camera becomes the source of an annoying second light in the eyes for another camera. The lighting and the camera positions are compromised. (See Chapter Eleven—Directing Actors for the Screen for further thoughts on how, if you restrict yourself to only two cameras, you can better approximate single camera setups).

The sound is also compromised, for the boom operator cannot get his microphone down to record nice, intimate sound, because then it would be seen in the wide shot. So there is either compromise on quality, or else little microphones have to be hidden in the set or radio mikes put onto the actors. Both methods are time consuming, **not** reliable, and neither sounds as good.

The **acting** however in the multicamera set up is done in "real" time—that is, the "Shhh" is the genuine and real-time response to "This is boring!" Some actors prefer multicamera, since it allows them to act in real time and for longer chunks. A normal multicamera scene would not be a short snippet like this example but would be a long scene lasting perhaps three to four minutes, with up to forty different shots in it, with the cameras whizzing about finding new positions to shoot from (in accordance with the director's planning) and the cutter/vision mixer cutting from one camera to another according to the shooting script.

There are, however, difficulties, as you can spot from the **adjust scale of performance to size of shot** thoughts on page 6. Good multicamera actors have to be prepared to switch in the middle of a speech from long shot acting to close-up acting. (There are those who don't do any of this, they just act the way they think. This leads to generalized acting and is usually associated with situation comedies.) There are many actors who, once they get into the swing of screen acting, really prefer the single camera, since then they know exactly what the shot is and can pour all their talent and concentration into each shot. In *Awakenings,* for instance, there is a shot of Robert De Niro with his arms open wide. In fact, there is a long shot with his arms opened wide, followed by a medium shot with his arms not nearly so wide. Good screen acting technique, Bob!

So there are differences in the way the acting is recorded, differences in the way a program is edited, differences in the way an audience looks at it all, differences in the number of cameras used, and—mainly as it affects actors— differences, vast differences, in the time allotted to shooting any particular moment.

Chapter Three

The Frame

Clark Gable
and
Vivien Leigh

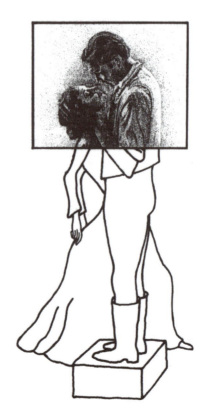

THE FRAME

When we look at a painting, say, a Rembrandt portrait, we do not wonder what is to the left or right of the sitter; we do not wonder what she is looking at; we presume that everything we need to know has been put into the picture—into the frame—by the artist.

Audiences of screen acting apply the same criteria.

We presume that everything we need to know is there, and **that those things not on the screen are unimportant or irrelevant.** This means that if an actor does wonderful things that are not seen, then it is as if she had not done them!

A frame condenses both time and space.

In real life, **or on the stage,** someone holding a cup of tea holds it about level with her navel. This is both for comfort and for convenience; it is easy to lift it up to the face or put it down on a table.

Putting this picture inside a frame means that the face is very small and difficult to see. To get a bigger face requires a tighter shot, but then it would look as if she had no cup at all.

So the **screen** actor holds a cup of tea (or a mug of coffee, or a bottle of beer, or a file, or a notebook or . . .) up close to her face, so that when the camera sees it, it looks real, we know what she is doing, and we still see all the expressions on her face.

(Yes, the cup of tea held high looks very silly in real life, but on the screen it looks very natural and "real." Have you watched some screen work and found similar examples?)

Don't forget, the audience believes that everything of significance is in that frame; so anything **put** there, even if it is just a teacup, becomes significant. A famous union leader in the U.K. has a familiar jabbing motion he makes with his hand when he is making a speech. Although lots of fun is made of it, if you look closely you see that he is keeping his gestures close to his body,

A normal
cup of tea

A screen
cup of tea

and in particular, close to his head. This means that whenever film is taken of him, he ends up with a nice, tight head shot. The camera operator does not have to loosen the shot to accommodate a flailing hand. I think this is skillful screen performing, getting a larger shot of his face, don't you?

This means that **acting** also has to be selective. It is not sufficient just to think or feel an emotion and put it where you think it should be. Just like the cup of tea, if you do not place it correctly, the audience will not see it, and it will be as if it never was.

This is why it is necessary to understand the size of shot and to adjust the business and acting accordingly. Ah, so you should ask the director, "What size shot is this?"

No. You should **not** ask the director, for she will think that all you are after is close-ups and will reply with such time-honored (and used) phrases as "**You** just do the acting and **I'll** do the directing, O.K.?" It is true that there are artists who care about being seen larger than life to the extent of demanding "another thirty close-ups." (Only stars get away with this.) So there is a danger that directors might assume that you are after such a mythical thing when you ask about the size of shot, rather than trying to learn your craft and using the best technique to get the best result. There are, unhappily, many who are suspicious of your motives and so don't mind keeping you in the dark about what is going on.

For size of shot—ask the camera operator.

Here is a big secret about crews: they all actually **want** the production to be good, good in different ways. The camera crew wants good pictures, the sound department is after good sound, etc.

If members of the crew believe that **you** are out to make **their** contributions look better, then they will naturally fall over backwards to help. No camera operator, for example, wants your fingers flicking in and out of the frame, so if you ask **her** what size of shot it is, she will gladly tell you so that you can decide whether your hands should be fully **in** or **out** of shot, but not wavering between the two.

Here is another secret about the frame: audience members sometimes think that **they** are the only ones who see what's in it.

Let me explain. Let's assume that in your scene another character asks you for money that you do not want to give, and your reply is filmed in close-up. Now, in real life, you would not let your face show how you felt about being asked for a loan, so a mild politeness would come over your face. This might be "real" in that it is what you would do, but it is not how you actually feel.

It is also very boring for the audience, which wants to know the **real** feelings you have. So in the single shot of you, when asked for the loan, your face can show exactly how you feel before the polite look comes over your face. Viewers will feel as if they have been let in on a secret, which they have. They will know how you felt about that moment—and will **not** notice that if you had done such a reaction in "real" life, the other character would have noticed it and asked what was going on.

No, the frame is an aspect of truth, never the real truth. Andrew Wyeth, when painting his "realistic" landscapes, would leave out windows of a house or move the position of a tree, because he was not interested in reproducing exactly **what** he was looking at, but in creating a more important and artistically valid painting of how he **felt** about his subject. This transmission of feelings is what art is about; it is why we like paintings and don't just go for a photograph of a place, why we watch and enjoy the work of actors, as opposed to watching real people. There **is** a difference.

Distances

Real people stand a certain distance apart when in a normal social situation (although this does vary from culture to culture), but they never stand as close as Clint Eastwood and Lee Marvin had to. In fact, we have to tear them apart to get them to a "proper" standing distance.

If we put a frame around the "proper" distance, we would then think they were aloof, and a large part of the screen would not be used. So the distance between them becomes significant on its own account, rather than reflecting a truth.

The close version of Eastwood and Marvin looked fine on **screen** when it was framed, but take the frame away and you would think . . . well, you just would not believe that these two men would stand in such an intimate position.

The same happens with Clark Gable and Vivien Leigh in *Gone With the Wind,* pictured at the beginning of this chapter. I do not know if he had to stand on a box or whether she had to bend her knees, but I **do** know that it is impossible for them to be in the framed position without such unsuspected activity below the frame. Her forehead below his chin gives a most wonderful **image** of the relationship (which is of course why it was so planned for, used and is still used as an icon after all these years), but in no way does it reflect what the two characters could actually do, or would have chosen to do.

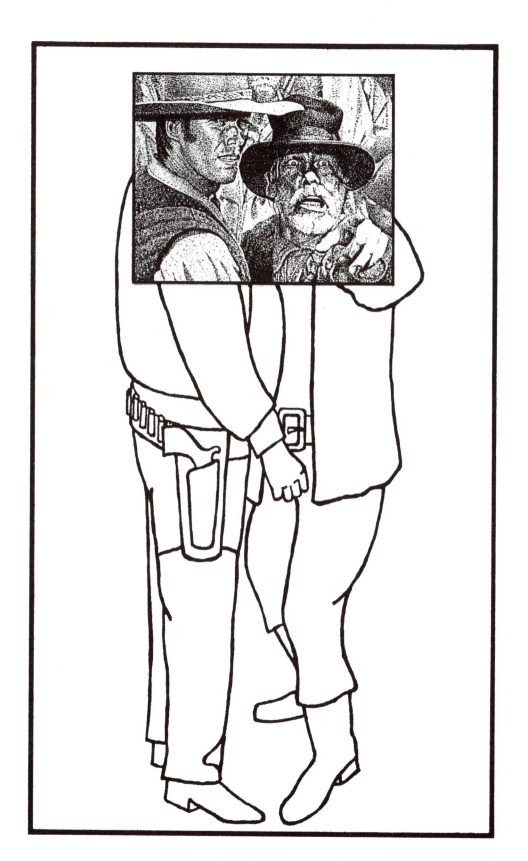

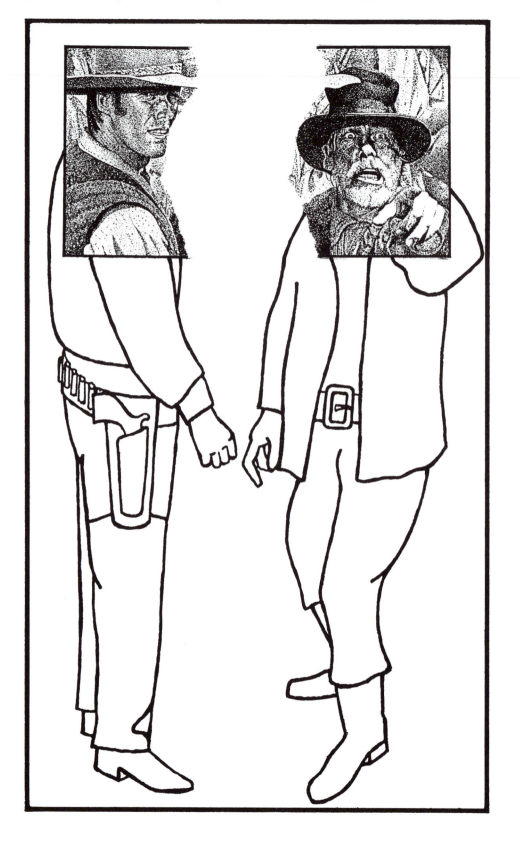

Film star exercise

Go on, try this right now. Pair up with someone (knock on your neighbor's door to get someone to help if you have no partner), and try to get in **exactly** the same position as Gable and Leigh. When you are holding yourselves in whatever contortion will be necessary, ask yourself, "How do I feel?" Your answer will be more in the way of pain and embarrassment than wild, unbridled passion!

This a very good exercise—to recompose moments from TV or movies, so that you can **experience** what screen actors have to do, rather than just imagine it. Most such imaginings are of an audience some distance away, drinking in your whole body's story, not of a large and expensive piece of equipment some inches away, with you sitting on blocks, balanced precariously, your nose one inch away from someone who could use a shower. Yes, that glamorous world can be just a touch uncomfortable.

Perception of reality

The addition of a frame alters our perception of reality.

Take a normal situation, where a person comes up to a stranger and asks her a question. In real life, or on stage, there would be a physical gap between the two when the question was asked, for a stranger would never come within the accepted "social space." If this were to be shot as a screen moment, the director might have the two stand really close to each other because she wants a tight two-shot. This will mean that the actor will **feel** one sort of emotion (**Why** am I so **very** close to this stranger?) while she is **acting** another emotion ("Can you tell me the way to the station?").

This is another proof that acting is far from "real" on screen and that, until you are experienced, you **cannot** trust your feelings; to say that it "does not feel right" is not going to make us flock around and sympathize, for we are looking at the framed picture, and if **that** tells the right story, then that is that.

Study dramas on the screen (as always, I advise you to do this with the sound off so you can see what is going on without getting distracted by the story) to see what distances actors keep from each other. You will be amazed at how close some have to be, and at how the distance can change wildly from shot to shot, even when the actors are supposedly in the same positions.

Not only is space expanded or contracted, but time itself is altered when a frame is put around things.

If someone asked you to come over and open the door, you would naturally wait until you heard the request before moving. But there can be screen situations where—because the actor making the request is shot in a medium close-up—it would seem to take too long for you to arrive. So the director might tell you to move **before being asked** by the other character, in order that you arrive on screen at a time that **appeared** right. With the frame around, audiences expect people to be able to appear sooner, and so they do. Watch the screen again for examples of people being able to rocket from one side of the set to the other—you will find them!

A lot of the mini-notes you get on the set will have to do with the **picture** looking right, not just the artistic composition, but how your character comes across by the way you present it on the screen. To understand why you are asked to do these little "cheats"—to be able after a while to predict them and automatically put yourself in the correct positions—makes you a valued collaborator in this most demanding craft. You can then enjoy contributing, rather than feeling that we are all out to get you, to prevent you from giving your best.

Group exercise

If you are in a group, look around the room and see what messages and moods you get from seeing everyone full-length. If you now videotape everyone in close-up, zooming the camera in and moving it from person to person, then play back the results, you will be aghast at how much is **lost**. When you can only see someone in close-up, look how much is not there—all the information that comes from what clothes she is wearing, from how she has crossed her legs, from her bodily posture: all gone. **This** is why I can boldly say that in a close-up, you sometimes need to do **more** than you would ever do in real life or on the stage, because the only acting instrument you have for this shot is your face, and **it** has to do what you would normally use your whole body to do.

Secrets of What the Frame Does

- it gives everything within it significance
- it changes distances
- it changes impression of time
- it gives an aspect of truth—not truth itself
- it breaks the link between what you are feeling, and how you are acting
- it encourages the left shoulder forward

An actor speaking confidently, but anxiously drumming her fingers by her side, gives a message that would be lost if she were shot in close-up, the jumpy fingers unseen. She would have to do more with her face to compensate for having no other elements to act and communicate with, if she wanted the screen audience to receive the same message that a stage audience would have.

Best shoulder forward

A lot of our passport photographs make us look like criminals or lunatics, and the common factor is that we are facing the camera with our shoulders square on. Set up the camera for a passport type shot, and then try moving one shoulder forward, still facing the camera, and see the difference.

If a character is facing us with her shoulders, and she turns away from us, we might feel rejected. She **ought** to be facing us. But if a character is **not** facing us with her shoulders, and she turns toward us, it is her choice and makes us feel good. And if she turns away, well, that is the way she ought to be looking, anyway. So an actor doing this makes the audience feel good about her. Also, if your shoulders are slanted, the camera can get a tighter shot of you without losing the edge of your body, and we know that larger shots mean a better chance of affecting an audience with our faces and feelings.

Since angled shoulders often work better than square-on ones, that is why so many starlets flounce onto the screen, then immediately angle their shoulders. (It also emphasizes their bodily profiles.) It just feels better, too, so the next time you are facing the camera for that passport photo, put your **left** shoulder forward, and you will get a better shot. (Why it is the left shoulder? It all has to do with the fact that we scan pictures from left to right, and that is dealt with more fully in Chapter Eleven—Directing Actors for the Screen.)

Chapter Four

The Camera

Marilyn
Monroe

THE CAMERA, THE LENS AND WHAT IT SEES

The camera is your Audience of One. It will almost certainly be more expensive than you, and probably more temperamental. Loving care and attention is lavished on it and quite rightly too, for without the camera there is no show.

A camera can pan, tilt or zoom. It can be put on tracks to dolly in and out or follow along; it can crane up and down. In a multicamera studio, it can do most of these most of the time. With single camera work, especially on location, it can do all of these—at a time price. I can easily explain the technical terms.

pan	rotating the camera through an arc; "pan left; pan right"; named after the long shots in the early movie days that slowly looked round the scenery: a panoramic view—hence a pan.
tilt	tilting the camer to look up or to look down—just what you would expect.
zoom	changing the size of shot by making it tighter (or looser) in a continuous way; it works by using a complex lens that can continuously change its focal length.
track	moving the camera on a set of rails, or on a smooth floor; it is great fun to use, and directors use it to creep closer, back off, and crawl around actors.
dolly	can have the same meaning as **track**, but also means the carriage that the camera sits on when tracking.
crane	moving the whole camera up or down, often as an actor gets up or sits, so that the camera can remain at eye level.
left & right	the camera's left and the camera's right, as seen by the camera operator; because an actor's left and right are wholly

dependent on the direction they are facing, we must use the camera's left and right, and this has the advantage that these are also screen left and right.

But all these terms only refer to what the camera **does** in a technical sense, and that is not what this section is going to be about.

Now for what the Camera does that affects the **acting:**

An imaginary acting exercise

Here is an exercise that I do with actors and students, either new to the camera or with experience behind them, **after** I have introduced them to the secrets of screen acting—both the ones you have come across so far, and ones you will come across in later sections.

I ask an actor to sit on a chair and act for, oh, about thirty seconds while I record the results. He can either speak something he has previously performed, something he knows by heart like a nursery rhyme or song, or improvise something. The person he is talking to should be just to the side of the camera. (This is a good chance to test whether he understands what "talk to someone camera left" means.) I use the microphone on the end of a boom to get sound, and I set up the camera to record a medium close-up of everyone.

I then charge through the exercise, being rather brusque and demanding (just like an unsympathetic floor manager). I ask that the boom be brought nearer, or put farther away, then rush the next person in after the first has finished (just like busy crews do to actors when they are trying to finish a shoot on time).

(You can do it yourself now, or imagine that you are doing it. Go on—thirty seconds for the camera).

I then play back the results. Oh dear! They all forget everything I have told them and go back to what they know—stage acting. Except, except that they are all rather stiff and formal. The vast majority of performers sit or stand there like butterflies stuck in a display cabinet. There is minimal movement, the head is rigid, and if anything of interest **is** going on, it is often in the hand gestures that, alas, are out of shot. To remind yourself about where the gestures should be made, go back to Chapter Three—the Frame.

When played back, you can see that many of these performers' faces are active only in the small area between the moving mouth and gesticulating eyebrows. The actor is only using about 10% of the screen to communicate with the audience. They tend, in fact, to do all those things they **think** screen acting is, the ones they have told me at the beginning of our acquaintance (do less; be still; keep it all on the face; etc.), and it is all very bad and very boring.

Whenever a camera is recording your performance, think in terms of how much of the camera's view you can fill with good, interesting and entertaining information. It is surprising how many performers give themselves restrictions that are not there, as in the above exercise.

In real life if you have something important to say to someone in a room, you don't say it from the hall outside the door; you go inside to give yourself a good position to deliver your message. In a similar vein, a stage actor does not deliver his best lines from the wings, nor from behind a sofa or another actor. No, often the only place for the actor is right in the center of the audience's attention.

The camera should be dealt with in the same way. If you have something good to do or say, make sure it is on camera.

If you feel that this is such a truism that it is barely worth stating, then stay on for this next bit.

When two people are on camera speaking to one another, and the shot is a two-shot (that is, both people are in the shot), it often happens that one of the actors cannot be seen well, because he is looking toward the other actor. I could, of course, also put the camera the other side of them and get a **reverse matching two-shot,** but this takes extra time and effort that would be saved if the first actor had simply **cheated his face toward the camera.**

Cheating

As discussed in previous chapters, there is a lot of cheating that goes on in front of the camera. Those who do it well know that it is necessary and do it even before being asked. They also provide a motivation for the "cheating" so well that the audience thinks that it is the **character** who needs, at that moment, to bring his face to the camera, and so the "reality" of the scene is maintained.

Two pictures follow. One is of two people talking where the person nearer the camera is not cheating well. The result is that we cannot see her face clearly, so we either have to put in another camera shot—extra time and effort—or we are going to miss all that is happening on her face. Next is an example of a well cheated face. Here you can see that although the impression is still given of two people talking together, the one nearer the camera has cheated her face around so we can see both faces, and so get messages and information from both expressions as the scene is played. To be able to do this, and to be able to do this so well that no one notices any artificiality, is the hallmark of a good and useful screen actor.

This idea of providing a motivation for the camera is quite easily understood when you think in terms of stage moves or gestures. A necessity (for example, a character needs to be got away from the door to clear it for an upcoming entrance) must be disguised—**cheated** if you like—as a character move, such as the character "discovering" that he needs to cross away from the door to examine a picture on the wall **just** before the other character comes through. The technical necessity is **motivated** so as to appear to be a character need. If you are cheating, then, it is necessary to make it appear that whatever it is you are doing is **exactly** what your character would want to do at that time—so in the picture the actor is disguising the fact of bringing her face to camera by looking at her tea cup: she has **motivated** the cheat.

The camera also "needs" a motivation to move. For example, if the camera is looking at one person, and is then going to pan to another person, then it looks a bit odd if the camera suddenly charges off on its own. Instead it looks much better if the first person gives a little look with the eyes or moves the head, to **motivate** the camera to pan from one face to the other.

The actor will often be asked to do these little camera-motivating moments. During a discussion between several people, the camera will repeatedly need to go from one person to another, and it works better if the cut occurs as the actors give an "eye-flash" to the other speaker. (See also Chapter Fourteen— the Editor.)

Often, the director will want the size of shot to be changed, say, by zooming in to a close-up of a face for a climactic moment, but does not want the zoom to be so blatant. (They do not seem to mind about this so much in daily soap opera.) One way of doing this is to have a character crossing the shot (for example, a maid with a tray of drinks) **just** as the camera is zooming in, so the actor's move motivates the camera to zoom in, the camera zooms as the actor moves, and no one notices the huge change of shot size.

Mirror shots

How many times have you seen on screen an actor facing a mirror, his face reflected in it? Many, many times, we directors, I am afraid, find mirrors completely irresistible. We are always arranging it so that the actor can be seen in many different angles and ways. But think about it for a moment. If the camera can see the actor's face, then the actor is not seeing his own face, but **is seeing the camera!** So all those loving looks and gestures into the mirror are

A badly
cheated
two-shot

A well
cheated
two-shot

not real, **cannot** be real, but are the usual cheats I have been talking about that make screen acting so very different from the realism some thought it was. Every mirror shot is by definition a cheat, and the actor has to pretend to be seeing himself; sometimes you can see wildly angled mirrors that are held or come away from the wall (a matchbox behind the mirror can bring it out to get the correct angle). You can now see it looks so silly, but the job is to make it look real, to provide a motivation so that it appears that it is the character, your character, who wants to hold the mirror that way and allow the camera to see your face in the reflection.

During that lovely moment in *The Apartment* when Jack Lemmon's character looks at himself with his new bowler hat and recognizes the crack in the mirror, he was **not** looking at himself but was actually looking at the camera, **pretending** to be having an emotional moment of seeing his new hat and then the cracked mirror: screen acting, **good** screen acting.

If you have a camera, try it out now, with the camera doing certain moves, and work out how the actors can help to motivate it.

A useful screen actor is one who understands the need to motivate camera moves and gives to the camera (all right, gives to the director, the editor, actually gives to **himself**) those little moments that allow the program to be cut together well (and so giving himself more screen time).

Speed of movement

A very common technique in starting a scene is to present a picture of a cup of tea (a glass of wine, a mug of beer) and tilt up with it as the speaker drinks, to reveal the scene. If a camera tilts (or pans) too rapidly, the effect is unsettling to the audience, so the actor will be asked to slow down that particular move. This leads to another "rule." Slow down **moves** so that the camera can follow them without bringing attention to itself. There is such a thing as a "television rise," when, to get out of a chair, instead of doing it normally—the natural thing is to lower your head as you start to get up—you put one leg under the chair and use it to sort of smoothly glide up and out of the chair. This allows a camera that is on your face to follow you easily as you get up.

This changing speed of movement is particularly applicable when walking past the camera, since the camera must not pan too fast or the scenery rushes past on the screen in an unnatural way, and attention is brought to the mechanics rather than the drama of the moment. This means that the actor is often asked to walk at a normal pace as he approaches where the camera is lurking, but to slow down just as he passes the camera. **Be very careful that in slowing down your moves you don't slow down your speech.** The rubric is:

Talk fast and move slow

This is quite difficult if your character is in a fast mode, such as being very angry. It really **feels** so odd to walk slowly across the room to grab your antagonist while words cascade out of you. Yes, it will feel most peculiar but **look** natural and wonderful—they may even say that the camera "loves you."

This love that is ascribed to the camera really, of course, works the other way round. Those actors who really love **the camera,** who play everything to the **Audience of One** that they know the camera to be, are the ones who understand the true nature of screen performance. Don't be confused, do **not** play to the camera person **or** to the director, just to that friendly little lens that soaks up all your best moments and is your gateway into the hearts and minds of your eventual audience. Just imagine that your Audience of One is nearer or farther away from you according to the size of shot, and **then** act naturally.

Because you are acting to the special Audience of One, even when you are on a set, you cannot always see what a fellow actor is doing. Even the director cannot be sure. There are many stories from the business like how, for instance, Laurence Olivier thought Marilyn Monroe was giving a nothing performance in the film *The Prince and the Showgirl* which he was directing. He watched her performance from sitting under the camera, could not see what she was doing and so thought her performance inferior. However, when he went to watch the rushes, all her wonderful talents were to be seen, and he realized that her skills included putting into her close-ups all those extra moments and thoughts that stage actors expect to do with their bodies. (In an earlier publicity shot of new starlets, you can already see this camera-loving quality; of all the starlets who were posing for a group of photographers, only Marilyn was quietly, confidently smiling right into the camera lens.)

Red carpet treatment

Because it is only an Audience of One, the camera has a very narrow view of life, and the camera sees in depth, not in breadth. The problem here is that all actors who have had anything at all to do with stage acting think in terms of breadth, of moving apart to allow the audience to see another character, to make room for the other actors to "breathe." For a camera it is all different. Imagine that there is a red carpet stretched out from the camera and all you have to do

---

Secrets of the Camera

- it is your Audience of One
- it wants you to cheat for it
- it needs to be motivated
- it needs you to talk fast but move slow
- it has an invisible red carpet stretching out in front of it

Real
people
talking

Screen
people
talking

is, wherever you are, **keep on the red carpet.** In real life and on stage when the group gets bigger we sort of stretch out sideways; for the camera, stretch out lengthwise—always keeping on the red carpet.

Try it out now as an exercise. Place three people next to each other, and look at them side by side on the screen. Then get them in a line, have the camera look down the line, and see the difference.

Experiment with positioning, and you will find that to get, say, four people on the screen in reasonable proportion, we need to stretch them out in a long line (all on the red carpet), or at least compose them in depth, so that the camera can see them all, nearest to farthest.

People stretched out sideways demand such a wide shot that we can barely see who's who. People stretched out in depth can **all** be seen well, the only difficulty being that the person nearest the camera has to cheat to make sure we can see his face when talking to the others.

More of this in Chapter Ten—Rehearsals and Technicals.

Chapter Five

Reactions and Business

Humphrey
Bogart,
Peter Lorre
and Sidney
Greenstreet

REACTIONS AND BUSINESS

Screen Acting is as much about **reacting**, as it is about **acting**. (I think it is probably more, but there is a limit to the amount of aggravation I should cause you at this point.)

In real life, when a group of people are talking, their eyes tend to go toward the person who is talking at the moment. Often the person who wants to speak next tries to give visual signals (such as raising a finger, leaning forward with the body) to get the others' attention and so get to speak.

In stage acting, the audience spends most of its time watching the actor who is speaking. If another actor draws the eye during a speech by a fellow performer, it is called **upstaging** and is not usually welcomed. (I once directed a stage actor who would mop his brow vigorously with a green silk handkerchief during the funny lines of his fellow actors, preventing them from getting a laugh from the audience. I thought this was a little peculiar—and so would you, since they were all in a play **written** by the green handkerchief waver.)

On screen, when there are two actors on the screen, one talking and the other listening, I believe that the audience watches the **listener** more than the speaker. Look at the picture at the beginning of this chapter—you can see that it is the combination of the talker and the listeners that make it such a powerful image. This is quite logical, if you think about it, since we can tell from the sound of the voice more or less what is on the face of the speaker— what we do **not** know is what the listener is thinking or feeling, and so we watch **her.** And the listener is often reflecting what **we** the audience should be thinking and feeling.

In real life, or in stage acting life, we will watch the speaker, because, although her voice may be indicating one thing, the story and message from her body language may be telling another. On screen, since we are often shooting so tight that we cannot **see** the body language, we will concentrate on the main unknown—what the **listener** is thinking—and that means watching her **reactions**.

Acting exercise

Remember the imaginary acting exercise in Chapter Four? Do you want to try it again? Thirty seconds of acting for the camera?

There is another fascinating result that almost always occurs:

Nearly everyone who does the exercise speaks, prattles even, for the full thirty seconds. Nonstop verbiage cascades into the camera. They all seem to equate **acting** with **speaking**, for given that they had only thirty seconds, they pack it with thirty seconds' worth of words.

They could have scratched their heads, "ummm"ed and "ahh"ed, started and stopped, drawled a few words out or given lots of reactions and few words. They could, in fact, have presented what they have watched **thousands** of times on the screen; but no, what usually happens is that they present uptight, word-heavy performances that represent nothing that they have either seen on screen or experienced in real life.

How did you do in that exercise this time?

Golden Rule—React before you speak

In real life, our faces tend to reflect what we have just said. We tell of a sad event, and our faces are then full of grief. We tell a funny story, and at the end we sometimes laugh more than our audience.

This is all very fine for real life; it even works well for the theater; it is **no** good for the screen.

On screen, a picture of one character speaking will be followed shortly by a picture of another character. The viewer does not want to know how the first person feels about something she has just said, they want to know what the **other** person feels about it. Since this is the unknown in the scene, directors and editors will usually cut away from a speaker **just before she has finished speaking** in order for us to see the responder **just before she starts to speak**. This means that much of what an actor does **after** she has finished speaking winds up on the cutting room floor. This footage cannot be used, for to stay on someone's face after they have finished talking would slow down the drama.

In the theater, this is the equivalent of doing any stage business **after** your exit line and **before** you exit. It never works, for it slows down the pace, and nothing else can happen until you have gotten off the stage. The golden rule for theater: nothing should happen after the exit line but the exit itself.

If the actor wants to convey extra information to the audience with a facial expression, the best time to do this is therefore **before** the speech.

Reacting exercise

Imagine that I have a simple speech to say. "I am very happy I was able to meet you. Unfortunately, I must go now." Putting my facial reactions in **naturally**, it might turn out like this:

A picture of my neutral face

"I am very happy I was able to meet you." *(Big smile reflecting that happiness.)*

A picture of my happy face

"Unfortunately, I must go now." *(Downturned mouth showing the sadness.)*

A picture of my
sad face

So—we saw a neutral face, heard the first part of the line, then saw a happy face, heard the bad news, then ended up with a sad face.

Here is a **screen** version of the same speech.

(Face breaks into a great big smile.) Editor/director can cut to your face during this, so the audience already knows your mood, wonders why and can concentrate on your words.

A picture of my
happy face

"I am very happy I was able to meet you." *(Face shows sadness.)*

A picture of my sad face

Audience wonders what on Earth has happened and so sticks around for the next bit.

"Unfortunately, I must . . . "

editor/director has already cut to the next speaker, " . . . go now."

Audience can now see how the **next** speaker feels about all this.

So you have hooked your audience into your upcoming thought—you have made them **want** to watch you. They first of all saw a happy face—wait, why are you happy? They then heard the line, and your face went sad—why? They had to listen to your next line to find out why. Dramatically more interesting, eh?

Yet again, I beg you, **do not believe me**. Instead, watch some more dramas on the screen to see what actors have been doing for ages but you have perhaps only now started to notice. Spot the reactions; spot the reactions before they make a speech; spot how reactions can be more important than the speech itself. Stars have been known to give away lots of their lines to other characters, quite happy for someone else to lay out the plot. What **they** want to do is to react to it all!

React your feelings? Or your thoughts? Or just react?

Here is a very **worrying** observation from a worrying exercise.

Choose a simple reaction, like swallowing.

Ask someone to do this whenever you click your fingers, regardless of what they are thinking or feeling. In particular, she must not listen to what you say but just swallow when you click.

Film the results, and then speak extra dialogue just before each swallow so the audience sees the pictures you have filmed and hears your voice saying such things as:

"I'm arresting you for drug smuggling."	**swallow**
"I think you're very nice."	**swallow**
"You've just won the lottery!"	**swallow**

The audience will be very impressed with what wonderful, truthful and subtle performances you have put on the screen, and so will you, even though you **know** the person swallowing was not feeling a thing—except perhaps a little foolish.

This is only an adaptation of an exercise conducted by the Russian director Lev Kuleshov in the 1920's, when he cross-cut between a close up of an old man and pictures of a coffin, back to the old man, cut to a skipping child, the old man, a plate of soup. Viewers admired the subtle changes in the man's face—in fact, it was all the same shot of the old man who had been asked to think of nothing, but the **context** of this shot determined the changes, not the actor himself.

In our context, a reaction is in relation to what goes before or what follows and is therefore not necessarily linked with what the actor would truthfully do at that moment, but with the whole series of events. In any case, many a reaction that is put on screen is not, in fact, done in real time but quite some time afterwards. When Gregory Peck takes his last look of Audrey Hepburn in *Roman Holiday,* and she goes off, he swallows. Now, when they filmed the shot of him it would have been some time before or after (if not another day altogether) the moment when she did, in fact, go off. So, was he "acting," going through all the thoughts his character would on losing his new love, or was he simply responding to a cue?

You see, it does not matter which is true; what matters is whether the **moment** was truthful and effective for an audience, **not** what the actor felt when it was shot. Another example from the same film came early on in the shooting. It was a night shoot, and the director William Wyler was despairing of getting a performance from Audrey Hepburn. (It was the scene in the car where she has to slip away back to the palace.) Finally, he bawled her out in front of the crew, reminded her that the job could be taken away from her and set the cameras rolling. We see in the movie her tear-stained face as she turns toward Gregory Peck with her final good-bye. Was **this** acting the moment in the script or a reaction to what the director had just told her about her personal prospects?

The movies are full of examples of "right" reactions derived from "wrong" motivations. But how can they be wrong if they work? They are only wrong if you still cling (are your fingers letting go yet?) to the belief that the actor's real feelings **have** to match those of their characters. In *Casablanca* when Humphrey Bogart gave the nod that started the confrontational singing of the national anthem, he had no idea what he was doing. The director told him to nod, and so he did. It was only when the film had been edited together that he understood why. Should that ruin our appreciation of his wonderful performance?

Listening

Much of screen acting is listening, and more is said about it in Chapter Nine—Auditions and Chapter Fourteen—the Editor and Editing. I just want to add a little exercise about it here.

I was working with an "elite" group of actors (that means they were all employed, and their names would be known by many outside the business). I was talking about positive listening. One actor was particularly upset by this, claiming that she hated watching actors pull faces and that listening should be what we would do in real life.

I immediately got her up to "listen" while another actor talked, and I recorded the result as a two-shot. When it was played back she was quite pleased with her good listening reactions. I then asked her to do it again, but this time not to listen to what the other actor was actually saying, but to spend her energies in giving a whole range of expressions. She did this, and I again recorded the result. Before playing it back, I asked "How was that?" "Well, it was **terrible**," she replied, but we all—the other actors and I in chorus—went, "It was **wonderful**!" Which it was. She was quite upset. "But I felt awful doing all those faces," and she was only comforted when I pointed out that **because she did them so truthfully and well,** they all worked, and it made for a stunning piece of screen acting.

I wonder if she had the nerve to do this again. And will you? Don't forget, the reactions must **appear** truthful and motivated, it is just that they don't actually have to be so.

Business (Biz)

Business means any gesture or action usually involving a property. Actors often use these occasions to let the audience understand another aspect of their characters, or to mark where a thought is changing. Although it might on the surface be what they would do naturally (pick up a telephone, open a newspaper), the **way** they do it lets the audience into the secret of what the characters are really feeling.

There are some schools of acting, particularly on the American side of the Atlantic, that feel that this is not "truthful," and they advise actors not to do it. What a mistake! You see her, the poor actor on screen, desperately wanting to show emotion and, having nothing to hand (literally), she pushes out her own hands as if in supplication—"please give me a prop!" You can see her "I've got an idea," as she brings her hands up to her head. "Let's put on a show!" and her hands stretch out full of impotent energy and longing.

Properties

Let's talk about props. Think of a pencil. Now, it is not going to change a lot in the next few minutes. It is an unchangeable object, but if you pick it up, it becomes a way of allowing the audience into your thoughts; it allows us to see how your character is feeling. If you pick it up delicately or grab it, this would show two different emotions and attitudes. If you wobble it about gently or stab it into the sofa, this would show two more. If you throw it on the table or break it in half, you have given more messages still. As you can see, a useful exercise is to see how many different things you can do with a pencil, all to help the audience understand and believe more.

Some years back, directing a simple scene with three roommates, I suggested that the stay-at-home should be drying her hair (after just having washed it) when the other two returned. This led to immediate professional jealousy: "Biz! we want our biz!" the other two shouted. Can you see the scene?

Actor with the hair dryer (entering and drying her hair vigorously): "Hello you two." (Hair drying slows down to a sensual level.) "How were your dates?" (Hair drying now speeds up.) "I didn't want to go out myself anyway." She was able to use the business (drying hair) to convey her inner thoughts (the sub-text).

Business (or biz) is useful for pointing up a performance as long as it does not junk it up. Here is another scene, where two staff nurses were scripted as having a fierce discussion—the one telling the other to stay away from her husband. How was I to shoot this? I set it in the small cupboard where the medicines were kept and did the scene all in one shot. The entire scene, with its back and forth dialogue and emotions, was punctuated at the appropriate times with counting pills biz, opening pill boxes biz, counting the pills in them biz, and swooshing them back into the box biz. The actors, both experienced and excellent, loved working out how to time which activity would match what emotion at any particular moment.

I feel sometimes that actors on screen should never be still, for the screen needs to be continually drawing the eye to its performers. Don't get me wrong, I am not talking of large gestures and moves, but very, very small, subtle, continuous activity. If you look closely at so-called "static" actors you will see that they are not, in fact, completely static, but there is a little move here, the eyes twitch there, the jaw muscles tighten there—loads of little movements which keep that flat screen image alive.

When we wave someone goodbye at the airport or railway station, we do not hold our hand up and leave it there. No, we wave it—and wave it for as long as the recipient can see us. It is as if we have to keep it moving to prove that we are still there, that we still care. In a similar way, reactions have to keep happening on a face—little shifts, little twitches of the jaw muscles—and it is as untrue to leave the face stationary as it is to have an unwaving farewell.

I had finished a television workshop in California, and some of the acting students were still a little unconvinced that this was true (still hoping for that "just think it and the camera will reveal all" philosophy?). As I switched off the video monitor from showing the output of the camera, it happened to switch to a local channel that was showing an old episode of *Policewoman*. As we watched (sound off, of course) you could see that her character was never for a single moment still—she was always on the move, turning down a collar here, straightening a belt there. The class laughter showed that they had finally taken the point.

Silent movie exercise

This is for those who want better proof of how reactions can inform an audience, rather than just relying on the reactions your character might "naturally" do.

Select a student to act out a scene as if it were a silent movie. Something nice and melodramatic—like standing on the castle ramparts as the villain besieging the castle shouts up that, unless she throws down the keys of the castle, he will put out her husband's eyes; she refuses, and so he does put out her beloved's eyes.

Get her to act it, and record the results.

Now, repeat the scene, but this time have the actor just obey the director's voice, and have the director (you?) give a continuous stream of commands: "Look down; clap your hands over your mouth; shake your head; suddenly look up; press your fists to your eyes; look down then up to the skies; scream; now slowly look down," etc.

Record this, then play back the two versions. It is almost **embarrassing** how much better the "directed" version can be than the "realistic" one. It shouldn't surprise us too much; after all, this **is** what happened in the silent movie days. And **why** was there a need for a director to behave this way? (In the early days of film it was thought that this talent of "getting a performance out of an actor" was the prime directorial job.) The reason is that, in reality, events happen too slowly and too subtly to communicate on the screen. Actors need to do **more** and **in a shorter time** in order to give an impression of "truth."

For a recent commercial, an actor was required to give five distinct reactions in three and a half seconds, and he managed wonderfully well. It was not what he would have done in real life, but was a speeded up version of "naturalism." (See also Chapter Nine—Auditions.)

You see, true human reactions can take between one and a half and two seconds as we think things through. This does not apply to instinctive actions, such as playing tennis, for there is no time for an Agassi to think for even a fraction of a sec-

---

Reaction Secrets

- react before you speak
- react while others are speaking
- the context gives a reaction significance—not necessarily the actor
- reacting can be more important than acting
- the use of properties makes reactions easier, and easier to understand
- speed up the gap between reactions
- practice your reactions—in a mirror

ond before rocketing the tennis ball back to the server. These reactions are only made possible by training, and the same should apply to acting them. What might take the actor a while (because he has to think it through) will take a much shorter time to the real person in the thick of it. For an actor to reproduce what the real person does (to reproduce Agassi's lightning reactions?) he must abandon **thinking** and go for instinctive reactions.

Because we are not trained or practiced in some of these fast reactions, we sometimes have to do them on cue, such as having a director talk us through a series of reactions very quickly (or shout through a megaphone). Although it will not be real to us, the rate of reacting **would** be real for the instinctive moment we are aiming to portray.

Practicing gestures

In order to achieve these sorts of skills and results, you have to get good at them—and that means research and practice. Research means watching yourself in real life situations and finding out what **your** vocabulary of moves and gestures is. Watch other people in the subway, in shops, at parties: what do they **do** that can be added to your vocabulary? Then watch screens, see what other actors do, see which bits you can steal—I mean adapt—for your own use.

I have never forgotten working with an actor who wore glasses when sitting in class but took them off to act. He did this in such a smooth way, rising up from his chair and slipping his glasses off his face and into his top pocket, that you quite forgot he wore them at all. This piece of business was obviously one that he had perfected over the years—and it said something about him. I am on the lookout for where I can give this lovely piece of business to an actor as an appropriate choice for a particular moment. (And I challenge any actor to be able to reproduce this speed and efficiency just by thinking about it.)

Humphrey Bogart was known for his sneers. He did them well, they were part of his actor's equipment. Did you know that he spent many hours practicing them, so that eventually he could sneer with any part of his lip he wanted? You see, he understood about reactions and business and made it his job not just to be good at them, but to be **excellent** at them.

Chapter Six

Sound and Vocal Levels

Richard
Burton
and
Elizabeth
Taylor

SOUND AND VOCAL LEVELS

This is the most important chapter in this book.

This, you might think, seems a bit strange, since this book is about screen acting, and you would expect the main thrust to be about the **look** of things rather than the **sound** of them.

I put this as the most important because, in my experience, the main reason why good actors are **not** good on screen is that they have their vocal levels wrong. Time and time again, I see a good performance (or a good potential actor) ruined by speaking too loudly, and the performance coming across as "too theatrical." In that 30-second acting exercise that you did in Chapter Four, you also got the sound level wrong, didn't you? You broadcast your performance loudly to the whole group, rather than to the microphone. Why do you think during the exercise I kept moving the microphone? It was to try to remind you of what it was doing, and how close it was.

Again, we need to go back to basics.

In real life we vary our level of speaking according to how excited or passionate we may be, **and** to how far away the person is that we are speaking to.

On stage, we do the same, but also incorporate how far away the last member of the audience is.

And on screen? Here, although the person we are speaking to may be on the other side of the room, the **effective** distance we should project to varies according to the **size of shot.**

When an audience looks at an actor on the screen, it is as if the person he is speaking to is just beyond the frame. So if it is a long shot, it is as if the person he is speaking to is about ten feet away. If it is a medium close-up, it is as if the person is three feet away. And if it is a close-up, then it is as if the person he is speaking to is only nine inches away.

Before you start to panic and think that you have to work out what size shot you are in, and what level of projection that should require, let me introduce you to your best friend and helper. It is not, of course, the director—it is the boom, at the end of which is the microphone.

The microphone

In most dramas, the sound operator will vary the distance from the microphone to the actor according to the size of shot, to enable the production to have "sound perspective." This simply means that when we see an actor in long shot, we expect to hear his voice as from a distance (and have a bit of echo or reverberation about it), while if we see an actor in tight close-up we expect to hear the sound in a very intimate way. These effects are achieved by varying the distance between the actor's mouth and the microphone.

As a rough rule of thumb, then, if you project to the other person **as if he were as far away from you as the microphone on the boom,** then you will be projecting at the right level for the size of shot.

How simple, how easy, thank you very much.

Does it surprise you to learn that it is not quite as simple as that? For a start, if you are using very little volume (for a tight close-up, say) then you will tend to slow down your delivery, reduce your reactions, lack energy and come over as very lethargic and downbeat. You must therefore **keep** your energy and attack, but **reduce** the actual volume, and that is not very easy at all. It is quite unnatural—but by now you should be reconciled to the thought that screen acting is not necessarily going to make you **feel** good, only **come across** as good.

Normally, the faster you speak, the louder you will get. ("How dare you—get away from my door!") If you take your voice down to a very low level, you will also be speaking slowly. ("Well, hello stranger. Can I buy you a drink?") To vary your projection level without varying the speed is so unnatural, it is hard to believe that this is what actors do, but turn on the television set, turn up the sound, and listen to what they are actually doing. A lecturer who talks enthusiastically and loudly, energetically waving his arms, will come across on screen as a theatrical ham. If he wildly reduces his volume level, but **keeps** every bit of energy and enthusiasm, he comes across as a television personality! Listen to a fast-speaking character in a close-up in a drama, and notice that he is not actually booming his lines, but hissing them. (See also Chapters One and Three—Stage versus Screen and the Frame and **talk fast move slow** thoughts in Chapter Four.)

As a further rule of thumb, the microphone will be where the edge of the frame will be, and during rehearsals the boom operator will be dipping in and out of the shot to find the edge. Do not always blame the boom operator if you see a microphone in shot; it could be that the camera operator has widened the shot more than in rehearsal, or the actor has gone to the wrong position, ruining the careful geometry between camera, actor and microphone.

You sometimes see microphones in shot on expensive films shown on television. Do not blame the technicians. It is because the framed picture for the movies is wider than it is tall (much more so than a television screen), and when they were making the movie the cameraman was able to put the boom in that top area of the film that he knew would not be seen by the audience. Showing the result on television, however, means that the edges have to be cut off, and to prevent this, they sometimes expand it up and down, and so show bits of film that you were never meant to see. Rather than complain, insist that your local television station show films the way they were made with the correct aspect ratio. (If that means a black strip top and bottom, who cares? It is far better to have that than to have all the pictures ruined by filling the television screen with incorrectly composed stuff.)

Directors and vocal levels

I have found that many directors have no concept of this whole topic. They will criticize a performance for being "too theatrical" when it should have been criticized for being too loud for the medium. They have even said of an actor that he "pulled too many faces" when, in fact, all the actor had done was over-project his voice.

When I watch certain films or television productions, I see actors talking to each other where the listener would not be able to hear the speaker at all—the speaker being very sincere, truthful and **quiet**—and no one seems to notice! That is because it **seems** natural, even though it is one of the most untruthful things that screen acting does. I have yet to read or hear an actor talk about this very important aspect of his craft. They **do** it, but no one talks about it.

If you want some good examples of this, watch Kyle MacLachlan talking to Laura Dern in the diner in *Blue Velvet,* or Jack Nicholson talking over the table to Shirley MacLaine in *Terms of Endearment.* In each case, the listener simply **would not have been able to hear** the speaker in real life, but in screen life it was just **fine.**

As Spartacus, Kirk Douglas is addressing an enormous crowd of his followers. We see him first in long shot with the huge crowd in the background. Then there is a cut to a close-up of him, and as he speaks his voice is so low that the front row of his soldiers would barely have heard it, **but we didn't notice, did we?** It was a classic example of adjusting vocal level to size of shot on screen.

Practicalities

The actual sound level "style" will vary from production to production, and from medium to medium, so a good rule of thumb here would be **never speak louder than the Star!** Find what the standard is, and work around that. A situation comedy is usually delivered with more actual vocal level than an intense family drama, but you should beware—if there is a studio audience—of projecting to **them**. They will be hearing the show via the loudspeakers hung around the studio, and so you should **still** be aware of where the microphone is.

Funnily enough, as the shot gets tighter and the vocal level needs to get even more intimate, there is less of your body showing, so the only medium left to communicate with is your face. I believe that in certain scenes this means doing **even more** with your face than usual (because it is the only acting thing left to be seen) and even less with your voice (because the shot is so tight).

So in the picture at the beginning of this chapter, Elizabeth Taylor should speak to Richard Burton **as if** he were sitting on her shoulder, and that is what you find she does.

I was shooting a dramatic moment in which one character fires a shot over the head of another character who then dives to the ground. I had him fall into shot in close-up, with the first character seen in long shot over his shoulder. They exchanged a few words, and I had to give a cue to the distant actor as to when to speak, because he could not hear a single thing the actor on the ground was saying (who, being in close-up, was only projecting to that level). They were acting away, and I was waving my arms whenever the standing actor had to speak, while he was pretending he had just heard what was said to him. Yes, filming is indeed a funny business.

Try this as an exercise. Give a speech that starts calmly and ends up with you in a raging temper. Put this speech on camera, and have the camera person start the shot as a long shot, and slowly zoom in so that the end shot (and the end temper) is in close-up. If you have a boom, this will mean that the microphone will start some six feet away from you and will sink to within a few inches of your head during the speech. After a few attempts, you will start to learn the trick of building emotionally as you get softer with your speech. But is **does** feel odd, doesn't it?

One of my ex-students phoned me in delight. Six months after graduating she had landed a part in Germany in the latest Claude Chabrol film, and she wanted to thank me for making it possible. (Such phone calls are most welcome!) A few days later she phoned me in despair. "The sound man says I am speaking too softly, but I think it is right for the size of shot. What should I do?" My dangerous advice was "What does Claude Chabrol say?" You see, there are some technicians who, to make their lives easier, will ask you to speak up, but it is **not necessarily best for you.** It just saves them the bother of getting correct sound. So, although you must want to cooperate with your co-workers, on this one I would suggest that as long as the director is happy, you give a cheery acknowledgment to the sound person and—er—carry on as before. If it really is too soft, they can do things about it, but too loud leads to you coming across as harsh and unconvincing. (Sound technicians can write to me at my private address.)

I beg you, **don't believe me on this one,** but watch the tube, go out and watch your favorite movie star, and listen to **exactly** what he is doing. I promise you will be amazed at the low levels used.

I was making this point to a regular director on the New York daily drama *All My Children.* She strenuously denied that her actors did such a thing: they just reacted to each other normally, she told me. I stayed on the floor to watch the recording of an episode (and here the actors have to do a one-hour episode each day of a five-day week). In each scene as the climax arrived, my friend the director (in her soundproof booth) was having the cameras get closer and closer shots, and—yes—the actors were building in intensity and **actually getting quieter.** At the end of the recording, my friend and I both claimed that what had happened was what we expected. She **still** believed that her actors' vocal levels were not changing, because to her, in the booth, that was what they **appeared** to be doing. I **knew** that the actors had, through instinct or experience, varied their performances, and in particular their vocal performances, according to the size of shot.

A small addendum here, especially for those in New York daily dramas: it is not a good idea in these fast soap operas to use the distance of the boom to guess the size of shot. Because the shows are shot so very quickly, most boom operators use long condenser microphones, and leave the boom at the top of the ceiling to avoid the dreaded "microphone in shot, we will have to go again" symptom. So the microphone is the same distance away for a close-up as it is for a long shot.

Radio mikes pose no problem at all for vocal levels. Just ask yourself, "How far away from me is the microphone?" And as the answer will be "about six inches," then you speak as if **that** is how far away the person you are talking to is!

Intimate speaking exercise

Here is a very good exercise that everyone should go through. Find yourself a partner, sit about three feet apart, and have an ordinary conversation with him.

Now put your faces about six inches apart and have exactly the same conversation, but only speak as loud as you would to someone that distance away from you. **Now** sit three feet apart again and have the conversation again **at the vocal level needed for the six inches apart position.** You have now spoken correctly for a close-up.

I do a variation of this when I am rehearsing actors, and they speak too loud. I just let them continue their performance, but I shove my face in and watch it from a distance of six inches. This soon brings their volume down (and maybe **this** is why all good screen actors use breath fresheners!)

As a wonderful bonus, whenever low vocal levels are used with normal speaking rates, because the actor now has less going on with the projected voice, much more happens with the face. Eyes light up and sparkle, the face becomes more interesting and animated, and character and attitude **pour** out of the face when the vocal level is fast and low.

Film speaking

There is a another major difference between television and film, and it belongs in this chapter because it is all about vocal levels.

A movie actor will do a scene many ways, not just because it is shot many times (as in going for another take), but because each moment will be covered from different angles, **and with different size shots.**

A scene between two actors could typically be covered in the following ways:

- Wide two-shot of both of them.
- Loose, over shoulder two-shot favoring one.
- Tight, over shoulder two-shot favoring one.
- Medium close-up of one.
- Close-up of one.
- Loose, over shoulder two-shot favoring other.
- Tight, over shoulder two-shot favoring other.
- Medium close-up of other.
- Close-up of other.

Now, moments will have been recorded in at least nine different ways, with many different takes of each way. The director and editor will choose the most effective, and that means choosing the most effective size shot that matches the actor's performance **and** vocal level. In other words, the film actor can do what he instinctively feels is right or what he judges to be right, but the **size of shot** chosen and used by the editor/director might well depend upon how loudly or softly the actor has spoken.

There are some actors (Marlon Brando is one) who tend to work better in medium shots; others (the English actor Tom Bell for example) who work best in close-up. As long as they are working in film, where there are choices, then the actor can "act naturally" and the shot is chosen in which the performance is seen to be the most effective. Sylvester Stallone, at the end of *Rambo First Blood Part II* in his climactic speech, "I want what they want—and every other guy who came over here and spilled his guts and gave everything he had wants," was not shouting at all, even though he was some distance from the person he was talking to, but his face writhes with intensity as he delivers the lines.

Again, go on—try to do it yourself. It is really difficult to approximate what screen actors do. It just feels so **silly** whispering, "and spilled his guts and gave everything he had" as you seemingly "pull faces." But it **is** effective, and until you try to replicate what you know they do up on the screen, you will be forever held back by an incorrect opinion about what "feels" right.

The unfortunate television actor, however, is often given only one size shot for a particular moment and has to make **that** work, whatever he feels he wants to do. In fact, I believe that it is the **television** actor who needs to know and adjust his vocal levels more accurately than the film actor.

Overlaps

One of the most common reasons for a shot to have to be taken again is "No good for sound!" A prime cause of this is overlaps.

To explain: if I am shooting two people talking to each other, I can set the camera up to get a nice tight shot of one of them, and the microphone can come in over his head to give me good sound. When this person speaks, I get a nice "intimate" sound,

Sound Secrets

- project only as far as the microphone
- adjust vocal level to size of shot
- never speak louder than the Star
- do not slow down or lose energy when speaking at a low level
- do not overlap unless specifically told you can do so

and when the other person speaks, a nasty distant sound. But that does not matter; for I will shortly move the camera around to get a nice tight shot **and** sound of him, and I will use **this** sound whether it is the shot of him or the shot of his friend. Problems arise when one actor overlaps his dialogue with the other actor; for this now means that I have nice "intimate" sound mixed up with nasty distant sound, and it is unusable. If an actor, then, has to overlap or come in on cue very quickly, he must leave a little gap between the end of the other person's speech and his own, and **in the edit** I will mix it so it will **appear** as if they had overlapped.

In other words, don't keep talking until you get interrupted ("Going again for sound!"), but leave one word floating in the air with the next crashing in after a mini-pause. Yet again, it will feel more than odd but will sound great in the final edited version.

Of course, it is absolutely necessary for the actor to know whether the shot that is about to be taken is to be cut into (in which case there must be no overlaps), or if it is going to be a contained shot (in which case it can be possible to overlap and be more "natural"). It is entirely professional to ask for this information from the floor manager. ("Is this a contained single, or are we cross-cutting?") I always tell my actors if it is a scene where they **can** overlap, for I find that most experienced actors have trained themselves never, ever, to come in over someone else's line unless they are expressly told they can do so.

Wild tracks

This is another name for sounds like footsteps going upstairs or someone turning the page of a newspaper. They are often recorded after the main acting has taken place. When they can be used, it is all due to the **low** vocal levels that work so well on screen.

Because the actor is speaking nice and intimately and **low**, all the other sounds getting picked up by the microphone seem too loud—the sound department's nightmare is a scene where characters are eating corn flakes, or vigorously examining a newspaper. Actors are often told to mime certain events (**pretend** you are doing the washing up) so that good sound of their voices can be taken, and the sound effects recorded as a **wild track** at the end of the scene, and added in at the dubbing session. Again, going back to the scene in the diner in *Blue Velvet,* you will be astounded at just how soft the background effects of cutlery, talking and other eating sounds are; completely unnatural, but just right as a background to the intense scene between the two lovers.

Looping

Especially for the movies, but sometimes even for films made for television, the dubbing session sometimes involves actors re-recording their lines again. This is known as looping, and it is, as an experienced actor claimed, your last chance to improve your performance. It certainly allows you to gear what you are saying to the way you now see the shots have been cut together. Again, it is the lucky film actor who gets this privilege (and can so make the vocal levels correct at last), rather than the television actor, whose voice will tend to be whatever he did on the shoot.

The problem here can be where the degree of intimacy with the microphone does not match that of the faces up on the screen. Actors often ask me why we can't just turn the volume down if the actor is speaking too loud. Well, we can, but it is the **performance** that suffers if the volume is wrong. When an actor is projecting to any great distance, his face becomes a bit harsh and stiff. When very little volume is being used, then his face becomes very much more alive, the eyes become more active—it is as if the actor, not being able to project his voice, is now projecting his personality. **That** is why it works so well. That is also why turning down the volume of the sound recording would leave the face stiff and hard, but for the actor to take the volume down opens up a whole world of sincere, vulnerable and effective moments.

Chapter Seven

Typecasting

ACTION MAN
CRAGGY INTEGRITY
DITZY BLONDE
INTENSE CHARACTER
POUTING SENSUALITY
ROMANTIC LEAD

Are they the
right types?

80

Did you hit on the right type for the part?

BACK ROW: Goldie Hawn *(Ditzy Blonde)*; Paul Newman *(Romantic Lead)*; Buster Keaton *(Silent Stone Face)*; Katharine Hepburn *(Waspish Lady)*; Bette Davis *(Tough Cookie)*.

FRONT ROW: Marilyn Monroe *(Pouting Sensuality)*; Arnold Schwarzenegger *(Action Man)*; Humphrey Bogart *(Sneering Hero)*; Spencer Tracy *(Craggy Intensity)*; Dustin Hoffman *(Intense Character)*; Jodie Foster *(Sensitive Waif)*.

TYPECASTING

I started entertainment life as a Director in English Rep, with a regular company doing different plays every one, two or three weeks. The actors needed to be (and were) versatile and wonderful—so I entirely disapprove of this whole chapter.

It is here because, alas, I know it to be all too true!

Suppose that you went out to the movies right now. As you buy your ticket, you look at the poster in the foyer, and you recognize **all** the names of the stars in the film you are about to see.

How many of those performances can you predict **before** you see the movie?

Most of them? **All** of them?

You see, I have not told you if the movie is modern or set in ancient times; whether it is a mystery or a comedy; whether it is set in Paris or outer space; if it was written by a genius or a hack. Yet you **know** the performances (or most of them) by knowing the names of the actors.

This is what is known as typecasting.

Imagine that there is a scene in a movie where the doorbell rings, the hero goes to open it, and there is the pizza delivery person, who says, "Here is the pizza you ordered." Imagine that the part is played by **you.** What will be the effect in the movie of you saying that line?

You might well reply that it depends on what you are acting, what you are portraying, what thoughts/emotions/memories are in your head. But you would be wrong.

Look in the mirror, and be firm and realistic. What message comes over from your face in repose?

Now **that** is what the message of your performance will be, and it will owe more to the packet of genes given to you by your parents than to the artistic/creative acting process you went through in preparing for the role.

Some people come across as sad (a naturally turned down mouth); others as cheerful (a naturally upturned mouth); as sensuous (a wide, wide mouth with pouting lips); as serious (thin lips), etc.

Go on—which are **you**?

Now imagine that the same process is applied to your friends and acquaintances. What sort of message is given by **their** faces?

Now you can understand how typecasting comes about. In the scene I have just described of the pizza delivery, there is no more to the part but the line delivered at the door. In a stage drama there is usually some description before or after the introduction of an important character; each person will get some moment or other to establish her character and mood. But on the screen? "Here is the pizza you ordered"? There is just no **time** to establish anything else, so the director (or producer or casting person) will, if a "serious student" type is wanted, cast someone who **looks** like a serious student (even though the actor concerned could well have flunked all her exams). If the director wants a bimbo type, she will cast a bimbo-looking person (even though the actor herself might be indifferent to those elements of life); if a psychopath, someone who **looks** it (though she may never even kick the cat); and so on.

Typecasting examples

In the movie *The Guns of Navarone* there is a scene where Gregory Peck and his friends have been captured by the Germans and are being unsuccessfully interrogated by an officer. Then the door opens and another officer comes in. The director gives this newcomer a close-up, and we see the high cheek bones, the white-blond hair, the "traditional" Germanic looks. There is no need for any dialogue, scene or descriptions: we **know** he is the Nasty Nazi **just** by the way he looks. You could say that his close-up **was** the performance.

The actor involved had no need for any inner life, motivation or such like; his looks told us the complete story. The director understood that the choice and type of shot, i.e., a close-up just after he enters, composed the actor's performance.

There was a famous Austrian classic actor called Anton Diffring, who fled to England when the Nazi regime took power in the 1930's. Once in the United Kingdom, he got continuous employment in the film industry playing, no, not classic parts, but a whole series of Nasty Nazis because that is the way he **looked**.

You see, in the screen world, time is at a premium, not just in the making of a drama, but in the telling of a drama. So you need a kind of shorthand, a quick way of conveying a whole range of information about a character, and the quickest and best way of doing this is, yes, typecasting.

I was once trying to cast the part of a doctor for a BBC play. Because I was still negotiating for the two leads, I did not know what was left in the budget for the part of the doctor, and agents were sending in suggestions every day. When it came to choose, my secretary handed me a list of over three hundred actors (including six genuine MD's who had given up medicine for acting) to consider for the role. I rejected all of these; after all, was I not a theater director with many ideas and contacts? I looked through my private file index for those actors who could do the role wonderfully and came up with forty-three names—again, far too many to be auditioned for what was only a smallish part. So I cast an actress instead. "Why a woman?" asked my producer. "Why not?" was the only real reply.

Again, looking for two old men to play parts in a drama set in a geriatric ward, I refused the suggestion that I should interview up to fifty old actors. No, I narrowed it down to six, since I didn't want to have lots of little old men trekking across London with only a one in twenty-five chance of getting the part. Then a terrible thing happened: **each** of the six who auditioned for me could have played **either** of the roles. They were all wonderful actors, some of whom I had seen years before in the West End theaters of London. So who did I cast? Who would you cast, and why? Not the best, they were **all** wonderful. So I ended up casting the short fat one and the tall thin one . . . "Aagghh! I have just typecast!"

There was a gathering of ambassadors in London to meet the Queen, and a photograph was taken of the huge group of them. An enterprising newspaper contacted several casting directors and asked them to send along actors to be auditioned for the part of "the Ambassador." They took a photo of **this** group of actors and published it alongside the picture of the real ambassadors. Among the actors were the little men with goatee beards, men with pot bellies, monocles and sashes, all the stereotypes of "ambassador"—**and not a single ambassador in London looked like any of them**. You see, they were actors asked to play the impression of "ambassador," not trying to imitate life.

Toward the end of his life, Steve McQueen wanted to play an entirely different role, so he sank some of his own money into a film of Ibsen's *An Enemy of the People* with himself playing the lead part of the doctor, a sort of anti-hero. For this film, he put on weight, and grew a beard. What did you think of his performance?

You haven't seen the movie? You haven't even **heard** of it? I am not surprised. The company making Steve McQueen's next movie bought it up and shelved it—no, not because his performance was so bad, but because they did not want an audience to see and remember him as any other than the crinkly-eyed, tight-smiling image that **they** had bought for their movie. It is called protecting your investment. That's the film business. (Robert Redford was once asked, in an in-depth TV interview, why he gave such an indifferent performance in *The Great Gatsby*. His answer was refreshing for its honesty: "I **could** have played the part very well, but I was paid all those million of dollars to present Bob Redford." Oh.)

We all admire and want to be those actors who **do** portray many and varied parts (Meryl Streep, Robert De Niro, Alec Guinness) but we end up—**if we are very lucky**—playing the same range of roles as do Julia Roberts and Bruce Willis. It is simple economics: a film is so very expensive, the last thing the money people want is to take a risk with a performance, so they buy the performance that they already know the public likes. And it is these money people who make the major decisions: not the artistic people, but the ones who have to drum up all those necessary millions.

What if the star is incapable of portraying a very different role? No one will know, for the roles will be chosen (and rewritten) to fit the exact image that sells movie tickets by the millions. What if she **can** portray a very different role, and does so? The audience, expecting the same performance as usual, might stay away in droves. Far, far better to insist that the director (and the writers who construct the part) and the costume designers and the makeup people recreate the role that made millions last time in hopes of repeating the trick this time.

The megastars are famous all over the world. Arnold Schwarzenegger packs them in in a host of different languages. Now let's think about that. Have you ever seen an American film with its stars' dialogue dubbed into Japanese, or German or Italian? Yes, there are all the familiar faces—and out of their mouths come these strange noises. Yet they are **still** stars, **still** popular, and **still** get mass audiences. This proves, does it not, that the attraction of the actors lies more in their looks—and what they do with them—than with their voices.

Recently I was watching a scene from *Twelve Angry Men* on Italian television, and although I knew the faces very well, it seemed so different without the distinctive vocal timbres of Henry Fonda, Lee J. Cobb and E. G. Marshall. What was interesting was that at the end of the film, there was a separate list of credits for the dubbers, recognizing their unique contributions. The actors in the movie—the American actors—were appreciated for their visual performances and for their visual screen presence: their typecasting!

Go back to the picture at the beginning of this chapter. Now, how many of these actors were cast for their versatility, and how many were cast with their performances already known? Of course, because they are or were great actors, their performances are remarkable—but within their types, not outside them.

Inexperienced screen actors

I imagine that if you are reading this, you might well be in that large range of actors who have little or no experience in the techniques of screen acting. If I (or anyone else) were to cast you, we would **know** about your inexperience. So if we did cast you, we might find that your technique was a little lacking, or that you might react badly to the pressure; your **performance** might suffer. No matter. As long as you **look** right, well, nothing can take **that** away from you; at least **that** part of your performance will be there regardless of other factors. So it is more than likely that for your very first part on screen, you will be typecast—even if you get to do different roles in the future—and so this chapter is particularly important for those of you new to the business.

In a soap opera or drama series, there can be many different writers and directors that may affect one particular character. The only consistent factor is the actor, and the one factor about the actor that will stay more or less consistent is the way she looks and comes across.

Interview exercise

Now you must try the most cruel-to-be-kind exercise of all.

Imagine that you have been interviewed for a small screen job by someone you didn't know—maybe it was me!

Imagine that the interview only lasted for thirty seconds, and, as you left the room, you saw me write a quick sentence on my clipboard just as the next person was walking in for her interview.

You know that I must have written a quick, short sentence about you.

What did I write?

Try writing it out yourself.

What did you write? What do strangers think when they see your **face**? What have friends told you they first thought of you when they first met you (before they grew to know and love you for yourself)?

Sit in front of the mirror, and look very hard. See the size of your eyes, nose, mouth, ears. See the complexion, the blemishes, the hairline. See the fat or the bone, the "character" wrinkles, or the baby-face smoothness.

And ask yourself, what would an audience think seeing this? What sort of character, what sort of message would they get from these, my special looks?

I am **not** saying you are doomed to play just the one type of part (although an amazing number of actors do seem to land only one sort of role). I **am** saying that, as a newcomer, you are **much** more likely to get employed for your looks than for your versatility. Most of the very big names have trouble enough getting variety into the roles they are offered, so further down the line it is all too difficult.

My advice then is use it or lose it. Use that nose, that chin, those ears—or get them fixed. Do not hope that they will not have an effect on what the camera thinks of you. Apart from the expected work on noses, chins, breasts and so on, plastic surgeons can now alter your lips to **give** you a permanent smile. (No, no one chooses a permanent frown.)

So, get known as good at your type, **then** with the experience you get, other roles can become open to you. But I am afraid that those siren voices that talk of range, growth and variety—**all** valuable and wonderful things—are not really addressing the reality of what is required of a beginner in the time-pressured world of screen acting.

After all, the history of great actors is not always the history of great versatility.

In Shakespeare's day Richard Burbage certainly did not play the small parts played by the resident comic. Will Kemp never got a chance to play the lead role of Richard III. In fact, in an Elizabethan play that has a scene where Burbage auditions an actor, the playwright has Burbage judging what type of part the potential actor should play from the look of his face and body, and from the sound of his voice. Do these thoughts from the 1600's sound familiar?

Back in the 1970's, we all enjoyed watching a ditzy blond on *Rowan and Martin's Laugh In*. We were sure that this was no performance—she just **was** the zany, scatty person we saw. The subsequent film career of Goldie Hawn proves that she **always** knew what she was doing, and the first thing that she did was to get very, very good at playing her image of a zany blond. The better parts came later when she was wanted, and therefore had more negotiating power.

Humphrey Bogart still has film series devoted to his work. Why? I think it is because, as a stage actor—although he understood perfectly well what was required of him in being cast in a film—he also made absolutely certain that his performance in *The Maltese Falcon* was different from that in *The Big Sleep* and again subtly different from *Casablanca*. In other words, **within his type** he found his variety and his versatility, and this is what I believe makes him still watchable today. He never exactly gives the same performance, but each **is** within his typecast range.

The father of playwright Eugene O'Neill played the part of the Count in *The Count of Monte Cristo* on tour all over America for over forty years! So no long moans please about how the modern actor, unlike her predecessors, never gets a variety of roles. I think in those days it was more often like today's casting methods than not. Only for the relatively brief period (in the whole history of theater) when repertory theaters were operating—from about 1920 to the 1960's, and actors were required to come in and play a different role every week or so—was the quality of versatility really required. Since this period is within living memory, and since many of the acting teachers on both sides of the Atlantic were trained to be ready for this style of acting, it is not surprising that they, in their turn, feel that this is the "true" form of acting and gear their training toward this type of performance.

As John Wayne commented in a television interview: "You've got to **act** natural—you can't **be** natural, that would stop the tempo. You've got to keep things going along, to push your personality through."

On a happier note, British actor Robert Lindsay made his first impact by appearing as an ineffectual working-class lad in a television series that had only six episodes. He looked and sounded the part and was then cast in the lead role for a series that ran for two years in which he played—an ineffectual working-class lad. Although he then had lots of offers to play (yes) even more ineffectual characters, he left television to play the part of Edgar in *King Lear* at a repertory theater. He had bought his theatrical credentials with his screen success. He then went on to demonstrate that he was a truly versatile actor (as he had been all along) and picked up the Tony for the Best Musical Performance in *Me and My Girl* in New York some years later. The moral? Get known first, get wanted, **then** think about where your career is going.

Film Typecasting versus Television Typecasting

There has been a change in the last decade or so, and it is interesting to think why. In the old days, the wonderful stars were turning out films for their Hollywood masters as quickly as possible, yet an actor like Humphrey Bogart would still only be in three movies a year, giving a total of about five hours of screen work for his Audience of One.

Profile view

Full face

A modern successful actor in a situation comedy on television, or better still in a daily soap drama will be giving many, many more hours of screen performances a year than that. This means that while Bogart could still give variations on a theme, Roseanne is herself the theme, and of course she is not expected or wanted to give anything other than the performance the audience loves and appreciates.

Profiles

Here is another exercise—not so cruel, but with very interesting results. You can do it either with a video camera or with a friend.

Set yourself at right angles to the camera (or friend) so that we see your profile. Go on! So many actors are ashamed of their profiles and try to keep their faces straight on to the camera, not realizing that **we** who meet you see this side of you as well as your full front. Just because **you** nearly always see yourself full front in a mirror does not mean to say that we don't know about the double chin, the lack of one, the "interesting" nose, etc.

At a signal, while thinking nothing at all, turn from profile to full face, and see what message is given. Yes, there **is** an implicit message, even when there is not any thought at all. If this is recorded with a series of people, then you can make it even more fun by adding extra dialogue when playing back the result, like, "Well officer, we picked her up for shoplifting"; "We caught him traveling without a ticket"; "She's under arrest for drug smuggling." You will find that some people come across as guilty, while for some, we all believe in their innocence. The look of individuals speaks a certain story, and you need to know what story your face tells. (Did they think you were innocent or guilty?)

The reason for different messages from different faces is quite easy to understand. A person with, say, an enormous nose would go from conveying a very forceful look—this huge nose cutting into the air, so to speak—to a softer image as the face comes around to the camera. A person with no chin changing from a weak-looking individual to one with, say, enormous eyes gives a completely **different** effect.

Now, there is nothing much you can do about all this, barring expensive plastic surgery, except to **study** it and learn what your face conveys in full front, in profile **and** in the change between the two. There are many actors whose most effective moments come when they slowly turn to camera, and now you can see why!

Try this as an exercise. Get in front of the camera, and goggle your eyes. Get everyone else to do this. Play back the results, and see the effect. Those people with enormous eyes must be careful, for if they goggle their eyes too much, it can look false. People with smaller eyes, however, can goggle to their hearts' content (maybe should goggle), and it just makes them appear more alive and interesting. Try the same exercise with licking lips, flaring nostrils, blinking—all the variation of facial movements.

From all this a simple truth emerges: there are no absolute rules of what to do with your face, for **it all depends** on what sort of face you have. So study it, get used to it, and get used to using **your** particular facial strengths.

Photographs

The very fact that you send out photographs is an admission that your **acting** can be judged by the way you look. I know that a great desire not to be type-cast and to be seen as versatile leads some actors to send out "contrasting" photographs. I'm afraid that very rarely indeed do different photographs do that—they mostly just look like the same person being either happy or serious (the usual choices).

It is often true that people go into acting precisely to **be** versatile. After all, the actors they mention when asked who they most admire are nearly always those who are allowed to be versatile (as I believe in each generation one or two are allowed to be). I believe, however, that the vast majority of actors are expected to present one thing.

I am **certainly** not saying that that is **my** position regarding acting. I **am** saying that this is the feeling of the profession. With all forms of drama getting prohibitively expensive, it is getting more and more difficult to take a risk—a risk that this person might be able to present a totally different character. If you cast someone who looks right (so goes the argument) then even if the acting is only so-so, or she falls to pieces because it is her first time on screen and it all becomes a bit much for her, then at least we have got the **look** right. Performances can always be improved in the editing stage by cutting you out of shots, or having you just looking over your shoulder toward the other actors. As in the example of *The Guns of Navarone*, your major contribution to a drama, at least in the early stages of your career, is often the shorthand of getting the look right.

Photographs you send out should do two things:

1. If I am looking for you (and that means not only the way you look, but also the way you come across—the "you that we know and love") then I must be able to find you just by a five-second glance at your photograph. Five seconds is generous. In some New York casting sessions they flash through a stack of photographs as if they were a deck of cards, and your images go by at about four a second!

2. If I send for the person whose photograph I have approved, then **that** is the person I expect to walk into the audition. Why bother to remove all those wrinkles/double chins if I will see them when you turn up? Why bother to have the camera especially low when your photo was taken, to make you look really tall, if I call you in for a part that demands height? It makes me deeply unhappy—vengefully so—when I am looking for a nightclub bouncer and send for you from the hunky-looking photograph you sent me, and you turn up at 5 foot 6 inches tall.

Actors are often in despair trying to find a set of photographs that suits them.

Here are a few things to remember:

1. Never forget that the photographer works for you. Don't let her dominate the session to the extent that you are a victim of her whims and style.

2. It is sad but true that most photographers make most of their money from failed or aspiring actors—let me explain—not bad actors, but actors currently not working as well as all students out of drama training who immediately get a set of head shots. Whenever an actor thinks her career needs a boost, the first thing she thinks of is getting a new set of photos. Most agents when they take on a new client will demand, as a starter, a new set of shots. This often means that the photographer is used to making you feel good about yourself, and this can sometimes be at the expense of getting you the shots that you need to get work.

3. The photographer will also often hide those aspects of you that you most dislike, and these could well be those aspects that **give** you your individuality, that allow you to be most totally "you." I once wanted a teenager with acne, and had to scour the pictures for an actor who I had to guess had this skin condition, for no actors owned up to it in their head shots. Another time I was trying to cast a dying man and had to plough through all the tricks of photography to find an emaciated face. When he came for the interview he had a scar down one side of his face—wonderful! It had been hidden by a shadow in his photo, but it would have made me want him **even more** if I had seen it from the start. Vanity, oh vanity, is a fence to be leapt over. So please—because the "professional" beauties are already up there or are currently being **manufactured** by the plastic surgeons—don't compete with **them**. Present yourself, warts and all. (You see, maybe we are **looking** for warts.)

4. Different photographers have different styles, and it is entirely within your rights to ask to see samples of actors in your type and range. In the course of your career, get used to what works best for you, and, if necessary, insist on it.

Too many "nice" photographs are only good for putting on your mother's piano for guests to admire—but will they get you **work**? Insist on at least six shots at the end of the session for you to do **your** thing, for you to present those aspects of yourself that you know get you work.

5. Often you will have a snapshot (it could be one taken many years ago) that you just love—or at least others around you love. Get this and take it into your photographer and say, "I want a professional version of this!" It will be a quick and effective way of telling your photographer what you want. I have nothing against photographers. They can be very nice people, and often their dominating ways have only developed because they have come across so many actors who do not know what they want, so they help out by giving **their** opinions.

6. I think that your photograph looks better if there is only one dot of light in the center of your eyes. It is possible, so if that is what you want, demand it.

7. Clothes tell an amazing amount about the sort of performance we can expect from you. A hint of a bosom "tells" us that you are well endowed; expensive earrings and a diamond choker "tell" us that you can play in an expensive environment; a torn T-shirt showing bulging muscles "tells" us you could play a street fighter, etc.

The photograph exercise

Here is a nice exercise to conclude these thoughts on photographs. Take an actor's photo, and put it on an easel. Place a video camera in front of it, so the image fills the television screen. Now, ask the actor to act a piece "in the manner of the photo." Everyone should join together in directing the performer. The instructions can be anything from, "Make your voice higher, lower," to, "Be more streetwise; have less intelligence," to, "Act younger/older," all these sorts of things. When it is

The Secrets of Typecasting

- most parts are cast with actors who have already shown that they can play that part

- your face already has a performance stitched onto it

- the image of a type is not necessarily linked with real life at all

- to protect their investments, the industry wants to keep actors within their types

- each generation is usually only allowed one versatile actor.

- actors through the ages have usually been limited to their typecasting

- get regularly cast as your type—**then** branch out

- if they send for you from a photograph, they expect that person to turn up

- if they are looking for you, they must find you from your photograph framed up on the screen, a photo is astoundingly explicit at telling us what to expect from a performance. Finally (and it can take quite some time), the audience will be happy with the performance matching the photo. Now, and only now, is the actor asked if she likes the performance. If not (and it usually is not) then she could be using the wrong photo.

The whole process can be repeated with different photos from an actor's portfolio until a match is found between what her photo "says" and the performance that she feels is most naturally "her." By using this technique, it is very easy for the actor to find the "correct" photo for her to send out, and maybe—just maybe—what alternate photo to send for a different occasion or job.

A final word about typecasting. When we go to an art gallery, we sometimes take a foolish pride in being able to recognize an artist at a distance—**that** is a Rembrandt, **there** is a Magritte, and so on. It does not bother us that the body of work by a great artist is recognizable **as** his work; we do not, in fact, expect a great artist to be versatile, but to be recognizable and wonderful, **within his own style.**

I believe the same applies to the artists of the screen and stage.

Chapter Eight

Acting

Laurence
Olivier
and
Dustin
Hoffman

ACTING

You have to be a bit worried by now that I seem to have addressed a whole lot of technical problems, but have not dealt with the central issue of "acting."

This is not accidental, even though the book is called *Secrets of Screen Acting*. But before we get into acting, we have to discuss what good acting really is.

I acted as a student in England and trained at a Method drama department in the United States. Since then I have directed theater and television productions in the U.K. and the U.S. as well as Canada, Denmark, Germany, Ireland, Israel, South Africa and South Korea. Since 1975 I have been training and teaching actors on both sides of the Atlantic. I have had access to, and knowledge of, a wide variety of acting and acting styles.

The result is that I find it impossible to define what a good actor should "do" in order to give a fine performance. I have known actors who believe and feel everything and who give stunning performances. I have known those who equally believe and feel everything who give rotten performances. I have come across those who have no idea what they are doing, who wow the critics and audiences with the truth of their acting—and, of course, the reverse, where the lack of belief and truth shows up only too well.

The one link I find is quite simply—**whatever works**. Some while back in the United Kingdom we were privileged to have working on stage and screen three wonderful actors—Sir Laurence Olivier, Sir John Gielgud and Sir Ralph Richardson. They **all** gave stunning performances, and all used quite different means to do so. The only link between them was that they were great actors. In the same way, I believe that his early performances showed Marlon Brando to be a great actor—no, not because he trained in any particular way, but just because he **was** a great actor.

Nowadays Marlon Brando does not learn his lines, but has his secretary read his lines to him over a microphone to be picked up by a concealed earpiece.

This allows him to be completely spontaneous with each of his speeches (and saves a lot of homework). Whatever works.

Laurence Olivier, pictured at the beginning of this chapter, had some slight difficulty with Dustin Hoffman wanting to improvise a lot while they were creating their roles in *Marathon Man*. On one specific occasion, when Hoffman came lurching in to makeup, exhausted after keeping himself up for days, and having run and run (just as his character was supposed to have done for the next bit of the film), Larry looked up at the exhausted, red-eyed figure and inquired sweetly, "Wouldn't it be easier to **act** it?" Whatever works for Dustin Hoffman and whatever works for Laurence Olivier—do whatever works for **you**.

There are quite a few performers (and directors, and certainly those who train actors) who are quite wedded to the belief that the actor **must** feel and recreate the feelings of the character at any particular moment. I am very wary of **must**, since I know that **whatever works** incorporates a large collection of conflicting **must**s. To explore this idea further, we need to go back in time for a quick dash through the history of acting.

Acting through the ages

Way back in the days when players started to get at least pocket money from performing, when the pageant wagons hosted the medieval mystery plays, and audiences gathered in town squares to listen, join in, and shout at the actors, there was little that was "realistic" about what went on. Performances were in the open air, in natural light, showing images and metaphors of life, rather than trying to imitate life itself.

When theaters became more established in the Elizabethan era, when Shakespeare wrote about "to hold as 'twer the Mirrour up to Nature" (*Hamlet*), and the best actors were praised, as John Webster put it in *An Excellent Actor* (1615), "for what we see him personate, we thinke truely done before us," plays were still acted out in front of an audience who formed part of the production. The audience always watched the plays in the same light as that playing on the actors; everyone was in the same room, and to see an actor was no different from seeing someone else in the audience. There is strong evidence that the actors addressed the audience rather than each other, for there was no question of fooling the audience that this was in fact a slice of life. It was a representation of life, not a replication.

As theaters developed, and artificial light came into the theaters, there was still no absolute division between those on stage and those in the audience, who were still lit by candlelight, even though the actors had slightly more playing upon them. Even at this stage, **the actors could see the audience**. This was an important factor in the relationship and the interaction of the actors with their audience.

Later theaters were built on a larger scale for the melodramas that followed the Industrial Revolution. These theaters accommodated a mass audience who wanted simple dramas reflecting the life they—or their parents—had left. (It was no coincidence that the villain in his black frock coat and top hat was dressed exactly the way the factory manager would be dressed, as opposed to the simple county wear of the heroes and heroines.) The theaters were lit first by candlelight and then by gaslight; the actors were still presenting their performances "out front" so to speak. They were concerned with presenting the performance to the audience, **not** in experiencing it.

I have experimented with the sort of lighting that would have been used at this period and, yes, you can see the audience through the footlights of candles and also through flaming gas jets.

(A digression: did you know that following a bad theater fire caused by an eager actor getting so close to the footlights that he set his trousers, and subsequently the theater, on fire, it was decreed that candles must be floated on a trough of water as a safety measure? Hence, in the United Kingdom, the terms "floats" and "the trough" are used for the footlights.)

It was only with the introduction of the electric light at the turn of this century that the blaze of illumination became so great that it was impossible for the actor to peer through this "wall" of light to see the audience. It is no coincidence that the introduction of electric lighting to theaters exactly corresponds to the rise of the so-called "naturalistic" and "realistic" plays. Now viewers could watch a slice of life, and actors started to believe in a "fourth wall" as the audience in a darkened room watched actors in a box of light.

It was the result of the actors being bathed in light, and the audience being in the dark, that led to the disappearance of the sensation of audience and actors being "in the same room," to each observing the other. So the actors started, oh dear, to believe that in order to be "truthful," they had to gaze into each other's eyes.

(See Chapter Eleven—Directing Actors for the Screen for further blasphemy on the results of eye-to-eye contact.)

When a new entertainment medium arose, that of the silent movie, different styles of acting were demanded. The camera (and audience behind it) was acknowledged, often directly, as the brilliant comedies of Buster Keaton and Charlie Chaplin still illustrate. Strangely enough, when the movies added sound, a lot of the skills and artistry of the silent era disappeared, and actors started to carry on about "reality," as if that had been the basis of all acting all along. As we can see, to "be truthful as in real life" had been the predominant acting style only from about 1908, when electric light was introduced, to the 1920's, when silent movies gained mass popularity.

The Method

A brief word about Stanislavski. (Take a deep breath now, and hear me out.)

The theater that Stanislavski worked in was based upon broad strokes, on a lot of "out front" acting and melodramatic presentational techniques. To these qualities the famous and revered director added his techniques, which are now known under the title of "the Method." It was a system that, **combined with** the existing ways of acting, led to the wonderful, legendary successes of the Moscow Art Theater.

Applying these same techniques, however, to those who do **not** have the same presentational background has led to some of the confusion about Method acting. (This also explains why such techniques work wonderfully well for contemporary plays but are woefully inadequate to tackle classic plays of any period.)

Perhaps we should instigate classes to teach modern Method actors the other side of the coin—the side that Stanislavski was originally on. Just as he developed a process complementary to what he found then, we should develop the equivalent complementary acting now—by teaching our actors to share out front, to make sure that everything good is shared by the audience, and to always know for whom a play or production is done. (I would call it "The Entertainment Class" or "How to Act Without Feeling a Thing!")

One of the best examples of this kind of performance on the television screen is that of the Muppets, who are not only believable, but also know exactly where their audience is, and play shamelessly to it. If you want to play Restoration comedy, I recommend a careful study of Kermit and his friends!

Modern theater, with its roots in small modern theaters and halls, with modern lighting that has done away with the footlights (and so allowed the actors to be in contact with and see their audience again) has, I believe, led to the growth of the presentational play, and the decline of so called "naturalism." The modern actor will often play knowing exactly where his friends or relations are sitting, and so his performance will be given in that light—and a successful one will use **whatever works**.

Whatever works must also include within it what the **audience** expects and wants to see, and that varies according to the period when they are watching the performance and the medium used to convey it. For plays written during the "fourth wall" period, then, of course, fourth-wall acting will work best, but for plays written outside that period (including a lot of scripts for the screen), other techniques should be looked to.

But what about all those classes on acting based upon variations of the Method?

There are so many really wonderful teachers and theories of acting in the United States—with its large population producing so many really wonderful actors offering themselves up for parts—while in the United Kingdom there are far fewer of both. So I have often wondered why, in the past decade, actors from the United Kingdom have won a disproportionate number of Oscars and Tonys.

I do **not** believe those in the U.K. are born better actors, that their background and culture is better for acting, or that somehow English theater prepares actors better than those from other societies. There must be something else.

Stand by for another personal theory.

In the United Kingdom, with very few exceptions, acting is taught to those who are preparing to be professional actors, at establishments that are not universities but drama schools.

In the United States, on the other hand, there is a thing called Acting 101. Acting is a class that is taught to a whole range of students, from those who want to become professionals, to those who take it as an interesting elective. The class must accommodate a broad range of experiences and talents, and the class must be able to deal successfully with those who have flair and talent, as well as those with only one of these, or those with neither!

Just as French 101 is not the best preparation to be able to negotiate a street market in rural France (but is a very good way of "teaching French" to a varying range of students, some of whom need the necessary credits and grades), so Acting 101 is good for "teaching Acting" without there being any necessary connection with the world of professional acting.

This is certainly not a criticism. It is, in fact, a praise and a wonder. The teachers of acting at academic institutions have to devise a way of teaching acting to students who sometimes have more ambition than ability. They have to provide a course that can be graded, that can take its proper place alongside other disciplines, and that must include the reading of textbooks for the course. Once there is a need for textbooks, someone will write them—and along come the theories and different "schools" of acting.

When it comes to screen acting, the authors like trying to prove that most of American Hollywood acting is based upon "the Method," and so there is a lot of comment along the lines of how brilliant Dustin Hoffman was to take all intelligence out of his eyes when acting in *Rain Man*. I am not denying the power of his wonderful performance, but to give all credit to the actor denies both the presence of the director, and of the editor who, I am sure, would only choose those takes where there **was** no intelligence in his eyes. If there were a glimmer of it, then that material would have been left on the cutting room floor.

Again, to claim (as some do) that Marilyn Monroe used her Method training in the creation of her role in *Bus Stop* ignores the fact that the director had to sit above her in one bus scene, feeding her every single line. This is not to distract from a fine performance, but it was **not** created in the way claimed; and in fact goes on to prove an earlier belief of mine that **whatever works** is as much a part of acting now as it was in the time of Shakespeare.

How can you give a shy non-performance student the confidence to go on stage and speak? How can you give someone with a great desire to act but not very much instinctive ability the solid background to be believable? Acting based upon the Method in its various forms is a triumphant solution for these classroom situations, and it is what accounts for this particular approach to acting, which is brilliant for its needs—Acting 101—but not necessarily the pathway for great professional achievement.

Perhaps we should leave the last word on the Method to Stanislavski himself (as quoted in *The Player* by Lillian and Helen Ross). Speaking to Vladimir Sokoloff in the 1930's about his famous book *An Actor Prepares*, Stanislavski says, "Sokoloff, if you go with Max Reinhardt to America, if you want to help youngsters, forget all this theory. Don't apply this. Don't pay any attention to this. Everything is different in America. The education. The psychology. The health. The mentality. Even the food is different there. We needed this book to open actors up in Russia. In America, it is different. They don't need it there. If they try to use it, they will unnecessarily spy on themselves, asking 'Do I feel it or not?' Tell them 'In America the actor is free.'"

I hope you are still out there, because the story gets better from now on.

Good acting—and good screen acting

My best friend was an excellent actor who had trained with me in Boston. Back in England, after becoming a successful stage actor, he got a small role in a television series with Roger Moore. I was delighted, because I **knew** my friend to be a really wonderful actor, and I thought that I knew that Roger Moore was really boring (you know, the one who took over from Sean Connery as James Bond).

I eagerly watched the result, and that is when the journey began that has culminated in this book: Roger Moore was much, much better than my friend. I was **so** confused: my friend is a better actor than Roger Moore; Roger Moore gave a much better performance on screen than my friend. Time to think this out.

Roger Moore may not be the most incandescent star on the screen (I think he would admit that) but he is a **superb** screen technician, and his craft at this is what registers, along with his good looks. If you feel I am concentrating too much on techniques rather than feelings, well, I think that that is what screen acting is. There are many books dealing with the recreation of moments of emotion but not so many (any?) dealing with the matters I am laying out here.

There are certainly moments in screen acting when it is absolutely essential for the actor to be completely immersed in the part: for the real tears to well up in the eyes, for the nose to redden and the veins fill with blood as the deep emotion floods into the face. Now that cannot be faked and must be "real." Yet these moments also have to be within the framework of the marks, the short scenes, the out of sequence shooting that is demanded by this work.

There is sometimes a serious undercooking of moments which are meant to be a recreation of life. For example, let me tell you about my friends, Rod and Lynn. He has always been a great practical joker, and goes to enormous lengths to fool Lynn one way or another. The time came when he was transferred from London to New York, and they were to move across the Atlantic for three years. Since they were both bicycle fanatics, he arranged for them to cycle to the airport and then fly to New York.

Meeting a friend at a party who owned a boat, he **then** arranged for them to cycle to Southampton, sail in their friend's boat to Brighton and get the train to the airport. Then they would have traveled to New York by bicycle, boat, rail and air. Lynn wearily agreed. Arriving at Southampton, they met their friend who, noticing the luxury liner QE2 moored nearby, suggested he take their photograph posed in front of it. This they did—and Rod then handed Lynn two tickets for the QE2. He had arranged the whole thing and had managed to get her there within a few yards of the boat without her knowing that this was how they were going to travel to New York.

A nice story—but why am I telling you all this? Well, the friend who was taking their photo in front of the QE2 also took photos of what happened next: of the complete set of reactions that they both went through after Rod had handed over the tickets. Now, whenever I explain the complete story to a set of actors, and ask **them** to reenact the scene from handing the tickets over onwards, no one is able to give such huge, committed reactions to the moment as the two originals did.

What I am getting at is that this was a peak moment in the lives of Rod and Lynn, and yet actors instinctively play it "cool," play it offhand. Most moments in drama **are** peak moments, and too many actors, by approaching it through **what they think they would do in those circumstances,** end up with a pallid, small and ultimately boring result. To do more, in fact, is to replicate what people do in real life when faced with enormous problems, enormous moments (which soap actors seem to do every episode). To reduce our reactions to "naturalism" can be "unnatural," as every actor who has ever tried to act out either Rod or Lynn for me has proved.

And don't forget, although a screen actor **may** be acting so well as to tweak your emotions, there is also the swell of music under an emotional scene that contributes a lot to the final effect. Watching certain performances without the help of music makes you realize what a debt is owed to some film composers!

I was having supper with a dear friend, Val Avery, in New York, and he had just put the lamb chops on the grill. (He is a superb cook, and I was really looking forward to them.) At 6:50 P.M. the phone rang, Val was on the 9:45 P.M. flight to Los Angeles, and he appeared on set the next morning at 7:00 A.M. to shoot his first scene. Now—how much preparation, how much . . . but do I need to go on? He was employed because he is a wonderful screen actor, and **that** includes his techniques as well as his talents. This fast preparation is becoming all too familiar and more common, as budgets tighten and savings are made in—yes—the actors' rehearsal time.

Versatility

This is a much overused word, as if it were the elixir of acting. Many claim the wish to be versatile as the very reason they wanted to become actors. Yet I seem to be preaching the opposite, that you should only do the one thing.

Not really, I honestly do believe that all actors must be versatile:

We improvise for two weeks before you get the scripts,	**now act.**
We block the play with its moves and business on the first day of rehearsal,	**now act.**
You are given extraordinary choreography and strange moves,	**now act.**
We do weeks of research, reading books, watching movies, hearing lectures,	**now act.**
Tell us about your worst fears, tell us about your father's death,	**now act.**
Hello, we haven't met before. Here are just your lines, you don't need the rest of the script, we shoot it tomorrow,	**now act.**
Here are the re-writes. I know it changes your character, but we have to shoot it in ten minutes,	**now act.**

The good actor's versatility is to be able to act under whatever circumstance of rehearsal he is given.

An acting process

And how about this as a summary of the acting process?

What do I want my audience to know and feel?

How can I convey this?

Now, let's make this appear believable.

And to illustrate this, I shall describe my famous sneeze exercise.

I interrupt myself with a big sneeze; I blow my nose into my handkerchief (and take a quick peek at it before squidging the handkerchief away). The audience looks embarrassed.

The whole thing is, of course, a big fake. I wanted to convey to the audience that I was blowing a stuffy nose, but could not do it realistically because there was, to be brutally frank, no mucus up my nose. The way to do this is to blow a "raspberry" through the lips that **sounds** as if you are blowing your nose. Now, by surrounding this fake moment with the sneeze, and with the looking at the hand-

> ### An acting process
> - What do I want my audience to know and feel?
> - How can I convey this?
> - **Now**, let's make this appear believable.

kerchief, the audience believes in the whole moment. Yet at the heart of it—the truth of it—I was not blowing my nose but going "brrrrp" with my lips.

What do I want?

How can I achieve it?

Now, make it believable for the audience.

To repeat the words of John Wayne: "You've got to **act** natural—You can't **be** natural, that would stop the tempo. You've got to keep things going along, to push your personality through."

"Speak as quickly as you can, act as slowly as you can."

"Save up your reactions until just before you speak. I shall probably cut to you then" (director Guy Hamilton in Peter Barkworth's book, *About Acting*).

Working with directors

(If you are a director reading this, simply transform the title to "Working with producers.")

More so than in theater, screen directors are time hassled. The clock is the constant enemy, and they are not happy to be engaged in a long debate with an actor who probably is not aware of the complete situation. Do not get into a confrontational situation unless you are more powerful than the director. He will not want to lose and can often solve the problem by sacking you.

Instead, ask the director for help. We are **suckers** when asked for our help, because now when we give a suggestion, it can lead to solving the problem, and we can gain praise and thanks. In a confrontation all we can do is back down, which makes us feel terrible, but help? How can I help you?

If a director comes to you with a whole lot of notes, **write them down.** This has several useful functions: It prevents you arguing back right away; it gives you a breathing space when you can read the notes after you have got over your rage at receiving them (and, who knows, some may be valid); and

At last—the Secrets of Acting

- use whatever works
- acting through the ages has always incorporated the audience
- Method acting is a specific acting style for a specific purpose
- real life is often more interesting—and larger—than our imagination of it
- a good versatile actor is versatile in approach
- it is enough to be truthful—but truthful actor/audience, not necessarily actor/actor

most important of all, writing down the note acknowledges your relationship with the director. Sometimes he is quite happy that you have written down the notes and doesn't always notice if you don't carry them out. (Once I had a particularly difficult producer who came storming out at me, "You haven't put all my notes into practice." I looked in my notebook with astonishment and then with huge apologies. "You are right!" I said and wrote them down all over again. I still didn't use them, though, because I thought I was right, and he didn't storm at me again. No, no, this is dangerous advice, treat it with caution!)

You have a different problem if the director does not come to you with a whole sheaf of notes, but seems to ignore you. Do not assume it is because you are beyond help, but realize that the director has many, many different areas to put his concentration into, and may not get down to noticing the performance until after the first take at the earliest. After all, the rehearsal and setup of the shot is the first time the director gets to see what the set/location looks like; the props and costumes and makeup are also up for his attention and comment. And then there are all the extras—he has to check that they are all doing the rights things. There are many calls upon his time.

An exasperated actor went up to his director and complained, "You haven't given me any acting notes." The director looked puzzled, "I am only the director—you're the actor." You see, he considered that his job was to choose and direct the shots, and the actor's job was to act. (I got a big hug recently from an actor in a soap drama. "What was that for?" I tentatively asked. "Because that is the first acting note I have received from a director in more than a year." Ah.)

Working with writers

Whether you are joining a regular series, or just playing one small role, it can sometimes happen that the writer has written the part in a neutral way until he sees what the actor is going to do with it. Finding the variations in the acting can encourage the writer to flesh out the script your way. Certainly, if you are a regular character, you can help your future development by "showing" the writing team what you are capable of. Really cheeky actors in a soap have been known to talk about events in their lives (true or not) in the hearing of the writers and then have shown great surprise when the same events turn up for them to play in their scripts.

But whatever you do, get skilled at showing suffering—remember John Barrymore!

Chapter Nine

Auditions

Paul
Newman

AUDITIONS

An audition is not just the moment of meeting a potential employer and perhaps reading for her; it starts when the casting people see your photograph and ends when you get back home after the audition/meeting/reading.

Since every actor has a set of photographs and is only too eager to send these out to potential employers, you have already accepted the concept of typecasting, that is, that we can get an indication of your acting from your photograph. Or, more precisely, we can get an impression of the type of acting you do from your photograph—the main factor being the way you look.

This has been dealt with in detail in Chapter Seven—Typecasting.

You can never tell when you will meet the person/people who will be auditioning you, so it is a good plan to get into your presentation mode from the moment you get within one hundred yards of the place where the audition is to be held. (Someone may, you see, be coming back from a coffee break and bump into you.) There was the actor who told the person she was sitting next to in the waiting room how rotten the script was that she was preparing to read. Since this was the writer—who had popped out of the auditioning room for a breather—this actor was quickly shown the door.

At the audition, you will often be asked to fill out a form with the most comprehensive list of your measurements—including such esoteric specifics as ring size, hat size or glove size. Have these all written up (and kept up to date) on a separate card. (They do this so that, when they do cast someone, they don't have to go to the bother of contacting the actor for her measurements. Of course, **you** have had to go to the bother of filling out all those forms, 99% of which will get thrown away and have to be filled out all over again.)

You will often have the vast excitement of entering a room full of people waiting to be auditioned and finding it full of "you." You will be amazed just how many other actors there are who look just like you. Do not be disheartened—after all, you don't know just what aspect of "you" they are looking for. (It is even more worrying, however, to enter the room and find that no one there is of your type.)

Be prepared to make sudden and radical changes in your appearance. Your agent—or the booking agent or casting department—can often make mistakes, and you can turn up all ready to audition for a "jogger" and find they are looking for a "doctor." (That happened to a friend of mine; he tried to convince himself and them that this was a doctor out on a jog, but no, they could not think further than collar and tie, and maybe even a white coat and stethoscope.) Actors—male and female—should carry with them the basic minimum for changing—a tie, a sweat shirt, classy or junk jewelry, a silly hat, etc.

Be particularly careful with your hair, since there are many styles that allow it to obscure your eyes. Do not forget, during an interview, reading or improvisation, that you will be seen from the side, and hair hanging down to hide what little can be seen of your eyes does not help your cause.

Do not be tempted to change your approach by what you hear in the audition/waiting room. After all, your competitors don't have **your** interests at heart, and even if they did, they could be mistaken as to what the casting people are looking for.

My advice is not to tell them your real age. If they really insist, then simply say that all actors lie about their age don't they? And then lie. I once was looking for someone to play a sixteen-year-old and was having difficulty in finding someone who both looked right and had the talent and experience to do the rather tricky role. An actress arrived who looked and sounded simply wonderful, so I told her not to tell me her real age—so she didn't. When my producer asked for her age, I was able to pass on the lie. She did play the role, and played it very well. After it was all over, I asked her her real age. She reluctantly told me she was really twenty-nine—but what was more revealing was that the same producer had turned her down a few years earlier as being too old to play a twenty-two year old! And you know, I think I might have been adversely affected if I had known just how old she really was, but I was happy with her lie—and very happy with her performance.

There are teenagers in their thirties—and certainly many middle-aged teenagers. Find out how you come across, and play—and admit—to **that**.

Auditioning for a part in a drama

If it is an audition where you will read for the part, you should have been given a script in advance, but all too often it is only at this point that you are given a script to look at.

Don't spend ages looking at it, trying to imagine what it all means and what the difficult words are.

Find out where your **reactions** could be.

Work out some nice practical business to do.

Practice positive **listening** for the lines that will be read to you. Go back to Chapter Five—Reactions and Business if you want to remind yourself of this aspect.

When you enter the room and meet the director, often with clients and agency people present, your audition has already begun.

A ballet dancer already knows how to do a plié, but she practices them every day. A musician knows her scales but still does them. A champion tennis player knows how to hit the ball and how to serve, but she still gets down to doing it every day in practice.

How long do actors practice in private? **And what?**

How many times do they practice walking across a room, shaking hands, and saying, "Hello"?

Silly? Hardly, when so many actors put employers off with a tepid, slimy, ill-considered handshake and a nervous greeting. It is part of their **job**, yet so many leave it to chance, leave it to the inspiration of the moment.

Try it now. Shake hands with everyone, say "hello," and then discuss these questions. Were some handshakes better than others? (Yes, they will be.) Why were they better? Carry on shaking hands until people agree that your version is good. It could be you have been going around for years with a handshake that secretly no one liked but no one was willing to tell you about.

Is your hand sweaty? Then have a convenient pouch with talcum powder in it. Do you have bad circulation and really cold hands? Then slip a hand warmer into your pocket. Do your fingers dig in another's hands when you are really trying to be firm and positive? Then practice different ways of grasping, because your handshake should also match your personality. A large handshake from a diminutive person, and vice versa, can be quite confusing, and the same goes for sensuality, toughness and so on.

The auditioner will often start off by asking you a few questions.

Why?

Because they **really** want to know where you spent your last holiday, or what your favorite part was, or if you put your face or your back to the taps in the bath? (Yes, I know that no one will answer "back to" except me, but I don't want a rational answer, I want the artist to get talking and emoting.) No, they want to get to know how you are when you are not "acting," how your natural voice sounds, how you "come across." Give them a hand: Initiate the conversation; tell an anecdote that shows off your strengths; **help** the auditioners get the information they need.

The moment has come for the reading. At this stage, they will often turn a camera on your performance, for if you are at all suitable, many others may have to view this tape. You don't know where this tape is going to end up, so make sure it contains excellent screen acting.

They will often position a monitor to one side of you. This is so that when you are reading they can look at you on the screen. That means, you need to give a **screen reading.**

A reading consists of two parts, both, I would claim, equally important:

1. How you deliver the lines;

2. How you listen to the lines given to you.

A good tip is to practice keeping your eyes up and listening to what the other person says, with full interest and sparkling eyes. Only when she finishes speaking do you drop your eyes to pick up your next line. (You can do this by keeping your thumb on your next speech, and moving it further down as you get to that particular speech.) Look again at the picture at the beginning of this chapter—notice the difference between Paul Newman with his head down reading the script and the version with his head and eyes up.

The person reading opposite you may seem to give an inexperienced, flat, monotonous performance. This may be because she is not a performer or because she has been **asked** to give a "neutral" performance, so that what you do will stand or fall by your talents and not those of the other reader.

Oh, so **many** actors, when they have finished one speech, pay no attention to what is said to them. Instead they frantically scan their next speech to make sure that there are no words they are going to stumble over, no words with difficulties, and to remind themselves of what the interpretation "ought" to be.

Why do actors do this? Why should I, the auditioner, **care** if they get a word wrong? After all, **I, the Director** am only too glad to tell them how to say it. And interpretation? **I, the Director** will be telling them that. So all that hard work preparing the text to be analyzed and thought about—who cares? Concentrate on presenting a fascinating, telegenic person, who, if she needs **my direction**, is even more attractive. (Directors love giving direction, love being needed, love having their skills used. Why not flatter the director by involving her in the audition? Ask which of two interpretations she thinks is the better? Ask if an alternative accent **if you do it well** would be a more appropriate choice.)

A word to the inexperienced (and moderately experienced) at being in front of a camera at auditions: your resume should tell me that you can act. I will read there what you have done in the theater. I can see you have done little or no television or film, so my one fear is that you will be "too theatrical." **That** is why, in an audition, you should assume that the whole thing is being shot in an ECU. After all, if you have done any theater, I **know** you can do the long-shot style acting, even medium close-ups, but close-up acting? Go to Chapter One—Stage versus Screen to remind yourself what this means.

I doubt if anyone has lost a job just because she was too intimate and quiet. However, many have been left by the wayside because they were too loud, too intent on impressing those in the room rather than coming across well on camera. They were too **theatrical**. See also Chapter Six—Sound and Vocal Levels.

If they stay to ask you more questions after the reading, be happy and revel in the knowledge that they are investing some time with you. If they ask you to read some of it again, pay close attention to **precisely** what differences they are asking for. They do not have the imagination (or the ability to convince their producer unless they have checked) to guess if you can do it a more preferred way. You must **prove** it so for them, there and then.

A different accent, a different attitude, something completely different? (That is my favorite to ask of an actor, if I feel that she has churned out something that has been carefully drummed into her, or if she has done an audition piece that I feel she has done all too often before. "Do it again, completely differently," I ask and see what **she** is about rather than her expensive acting coach or "helpful friend.") Be particularly careful, if given something different to do, that you don't get louder. My experience is that a wonderful close-up version of a reading suddenly goes into back of the balcony when the actor is asked for a different accent or attitude.

Whatever you do, do not fall into the trap of being more entertaining in the interview than you are in the reading. If you are vivacious, funny and bubbly, and then give a cold, quiet, little reading, we will feel a little let down, a little cheated. Play to your strengths, so if you are a laughing happy type, play the part putting in some of your natural personality. After all, there must be a reason why the casting people chose you from a submitted photograph or why your agent put you up for the job. Too many actors start to play, say, gruff when they are naturally light-hearted performers, and vice versa.

Margot Stevenson looks just like the owner of Tweety-Pie (the cartoon canary that Sylvester the cat is always trying to munch). She had just returned from a commercial casting session where she was auditioning for a granny type of role. I asked her to do for me what she had done for the audition. She played a gruff, angry granny, but she is a most wonderful, cheerful, apple-cheeked, **happy** granny. When I made her do it again in her **own** manner and style, the reading took off and blossomed. "Why didn't I do that the first time?" she mused. But of course she was acting what she thought they wanted, an angry granny, rather than presenting her strengths and specialties.

So if this is one of those auditions where you seem to have been sent to the wrong place, where they are looking for a "student" type and you come across as a young parent; or a flashy blonde seems to be what everyone else in the room is, and you are a quiet brunette, do not try to compete with the other actors on their own terms. After all, they have had many years to practice this. Concentrate on **your** image and personality, and convince the auditioners that maybe **you** are what they are looking for. Don't attempt something that is not one of your positives. As I said in Chapter Seven—Typecasting, **always** play to your strengths.

Auditioning for a drama, be prepared to

- be on best behavior
- change appearance
- practice a good greeting
- lie about your age
- prepare reactions as much as the text
- act as if in Extreme Close-Up
- exit gracefully

The auditioners usually have many people to see, so don't overstay your welcome. Sometimes—it's not your fault—they know from the moment you come in that you will not be right. You should concentrate on making a snappy impact, and then get out quickly. This makes us like you, for it gives us time to go to the bathroom or have a cup of coffee.

Give yourself a good exit. Nothing is worse than making a good impression with your reading and then slinking off. **Do not** groan, moan or utter cries of anguish in the corridor. It is very off-putting for us to hear (for we do) someone indicating that the occasion of meeting us was so very painful.

I once auditioned a young actor, and all went well. After he left, my secretary said, "There goes a happy actor." I looked out of the window, and there he was, leaping over the fences in the park and crazily making his way off. He had obviously enjoyed meeting me.

He got the job.

Auditioning for a commercial

At these auditions you can be surprised at how many people will be called in, or how long the audition has gone on for a part that is, frankly, just a look and a smile.

The audition will most likely be with a casting person and a camera.

The producer/director could well be thousands of miles away, and will be sent a videotape of the "best" results. This can mean that, if you get the job, they might expect to see the same type of clothes you wore to the audition. A friend of mine got into trouble because, cast in a commercial, he smartened himself up by getting a haircut—and they had cast him **because** of the lock of hair that fell across his face.

Actors need to be able to produce what is required remarkably quickly. In Europe, a lot of the commercials are cast and made using actors from the U.K. It is not just because British actors are cheaper, it is because they are faster. They don't waste time asking about motivation or waiting until they "feel right" before going for a take. They just get on with it.

You can be asked to do something as small as,"Say your name and agent to the camera, and then eat a piece of chocolate and say, 'Wow!'"

It can be as long as doing a complicated improvisation with a fellow actor, where you act up a storm doing and saying wonderful things, and those auditioning you write down the best lines they hear. (They couldn't possibly do this, could they? That would be stealing your ideas!)

How often have you practiced saying your name and agent into a camera? You can guess the rest of my argument: if a ballet dancer practices at the bar every morning. . . . There is a serious point to this, though. Since the videotape of your audition (and the hundred or so others they saw that day) could well be sent on to the producer or director elsewhere, if they do not like the way you introduce yourself, well, there is always the fast forward button. They might never even get to see your wonderful reading—your dull introduction would have put them off.

And yet, too many actors are really indifferent to this, the first impression you are going to give on a tape that will be watched by someone in different circumstances, thinking different thoughts. By using **this** moment to give us an impression of "you," then your subsequent audition can be a chance to show a second variation on what you are about.

So many actors are quite timid and small on doing a "wow," or in giving a **big** reaction to "seeing" something, but that is what is required in the split-second world of commercials. It always surprises me that actors who, along with the rest of the population, have seen **thousands** of commercials with these clear, positive reactions, are so timid when reproducing it themselves. It is as if they had never truly sat down and watched what it is that they themselves would like to do at some time in their careers. (Financing a season of acting in the theater via a few good commercials is a very acceptable way of running a career.)

Here is an inexperienced "Wow!" followed by an experienced one. Which do you prefer? Can you be as committed as the experienced one?

They are not looking for someone who quite likes their product and thinks it is the best chocolate she has eaten this week. They are not looking for someone who, with her "Wow!" shows that this is the best chocolate she has eaten this year. They are looking for someone who will radiate that this is the very, **very** best chocolate she has ever, **ever** eaten. It is an extreme that they are looking for, and if you do not give it, there are many other people lined up outside the door who will want to give it **their** best shot.

Deeply committed emotions are not all that is required, timings need to be extreme as well. There is a very good commercial in the U.K. (for Carlsberg lager) where a customs official looks up with glee at the prospect of catching travelers returning from Denmark, laden with that particular beer. In close-up, his face (and I timed it) did five distinct reactions in three and a half seconds. Now **that** is good screen acting and very difficult to do. Try it yourself—**now**—to see that this requires **technique**, like so much else.

Sometimes at an audition they investigate your talents by giving you an improvisation that is based upon the circumstances in the commercial without performing it exactly. In such an improvised scene, remember where the camera is, and keep close to your partner, so that the shot can always be the tightest two-shot of both of you, and so that your faces will be correspondingly larger. Again, inexperienced actors position themselves as if on a mini-stage. They keep a horizontal distance between each other, necessitating a

An
inexperienced
"Wow!"

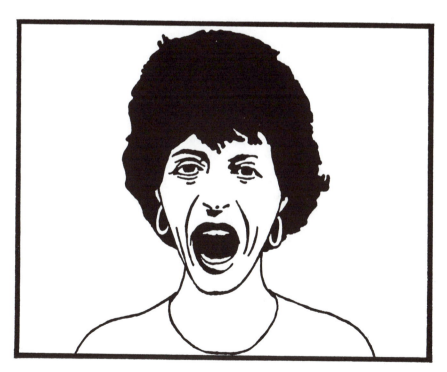

An
experienced
"Wow!"

very **wide** shot, and resulting in a correspondingly very **small** shot of their expressive faces. Remember, it is not what you **feel**, but what the camera **sees** that counts.

Often, at these improvisations, they do not record the sound at all. They already have expensive, skilled copywriters and are interested in the actor's skill at transmitting emotions, not in inventing dialogue. So don't spend too much of your energy trying to be witty—treat it like a silent movie and put your skills and talent into visual moments.

Talent versus results

I suppose the biggest difference between auditions for the screen and for the stage is that for the stage they are often looking for talent, looking for potential. The stage audition is to find out those who—with rehearsal—can give excellent performances. For the screen, and particularly for commercials, they are not looking for talent or for potential: they are looking for results. It is as if the audition is the job itself, and they are looking for someone who, if she is chosen, will be expected to do exactly the same at the shoot as she did at the audition. Treat the audition, then, as the job itself. Although casting people and directors know that actors have potential and can improve with work, the advertising executives and all manner of people who actually decide who will be the face for the commercial can only judge by what they see.

My partner went for a commercial audition that included a photo session, and they asked her for lots of different expressions. She did so, and they took seven Polaroid shots of her. She got the job, and when she turned up for the studio session, the professional photographer they had hired to take the pictures had on his storyboard (a rough drawing of what the advertisers wanted) **six** of the original Polaroids taken at the audition. He and the actor were not supposed to create magic, to create some wonderful pictures that matched the copywriters' ideas: they were to **recreate what had happened in the audition.**

This happens so often because—although the casting director and director can imagine how an actor might be in different circumstances, after a little direction and so on—the clients cannot. **They** think that what they see is all they are going to get, and so they choose actors for results, not for potential.

So what happens if you commit yourself to a performance that does not fit into their preconceived idea? Well, if you do it well, with deep conviction, you might change their minds. It is possible (likely?) that you won't get the job, but if you have impressed the casting director, then you still have the future.

Not getting the job

Now, there are a lot of jobs you are not going to get. You should **hope** that there are a lot of jobs you are not going to get, because that means that you are going for a lot of auditions. Do not work yourself up into a lather of expectation about a particular audition, declaring "This is it!" and setting yourself up for a major trauma when the job does not come your way. There are many, many reasons why you may not get a job, one of which may be that there was no job in the first place; it had already been cast. Why should we audition if we know the part has already gone? Insurance, union necessity, because the room is booked, and it is cheaper to audition than let everyone know not to come—there are **lots** of good reasons.

Then again, your hair may be the wrong color. No, don't shout that you will dye it. It is quicker and easier to get someone with the right hair (which must not be exactly the same as the star's, otherwise the audience will get confused) than to risk a wig or dye job. Also, the bright lights needed for shooting sometimes make false colors look odd. Usually a wig is more expensive than an actor, and I would prefer using two actors rather than just you plus the cost of a wig.

It is just possible you might not get the job because you would overshadow someone else in the cast. Putting a cast together is sometimes an instinctive process that does not bear logical study. However, we do feel sad for those not cast and would hate to say that you didn't get the part because, well, just because. So we add "reasons" hoping you will feel better, like: too old, too young, too tall, too short, too blond, too dark. Anyone who has auditioned can add to this long list. These are not the **real** reasons, but the trouble is that actors seize upon these little snippets and put a religious certainty upon them, trying to solve what they **thought** was the reason for not being cast. Actors have made themselves ill taking seriously a little comment that was only said to make them feel better.

You didn't get cast? Oh well, it would have been nice; now on to the next. The only strong advice I would remind you of again is: **never be more interesting in the interview than in the reading.**

(There is a lot of good stuff about auditions in the book *Getting the Part* listed in the Bibliography.)

Casting directors

Sometimes these creatures seem to be an impenetrable barrier between you and a job, but you should instead look upon them as part of the process, a part you need to get along with.

Many casting directors will not interview actors individually, but will add the odd unknown actor to a casting session to see how she does. Oh, they have no belief that you will actually get the job, but it gives them a chance to see how you act under these conditions and how you come across.

If you come across well, then it is good for their reputations to call you up, even if you are not quite right for the job. A friend of mine was sent to casting sessions for ten years by a particular casting director, before she actually landed a job from one of them. Her auditions had always been good, but none of the commercials had come through because, well, because there are so many people auditioning and just so many parts. She jokingly apologized to him for never getting the job. "Don't worry," he replied, "the clients always **love** you." And that is why he kept sending for her, because she always gave a good account of herself and never let the casting director down.

Add to the process the throng of casting, advising, account executives and advertising managers, who **all** contribute to who they think should be the "face" that sells a particular product, and there are many fences to fall at. Don't forget, delivering a good performance at auditions throws credit onto the casting director, who you may well need later on in your career.

To be depressed at not getting a job for some while is understandable, but it is not necessarily a criticism of your ability. It is certainly **not** true that you will definitely make it if you are really talented. This is a myth circulated by those who **have** made it, to prove that they themselves must have talent. I know a lot of really talented actors whose expertise has not been used to the full—and I am sure **you** know of people whose achievements are greater than their abilities.

The casting director may well cast both dramas and commercials, so be sure to make a very good impression—even if it is for a commercial for a product that you neither believe in, or would rather not be asked to do due to political or environmental considerations.

Auditioning for a commercial, be prepared to

- do the same as for a drama audition
- give really committed reactions
- show results, not just potential
- keep from getting depressed at the constant rejections

Another word about casting—and an answer to those stories you have heard about someone being cast by being seen serving behind the counter at Woolworth's. If you were to audition enough people, you would by accident alone find someone who could act one particular part. The casting of Macaulay Culkin, the star of *Home Alone*, was the result of many, many auditions. It is only **now** that he gets chosen before the script is written; up to then it was: here is the script, now let's go out there and find someone. If you audition a whole room of inexperienced screen actors, then some, just by accident, will manage to "come across" on the screen better than others—and that is how I believe a whole lot of casting has happened in the past.

We no longer accept that theater actors "just happen" and we acknowledge that training is an important part of getting ready for performing on stage. I believe it is the same for the screen. If a magic wand were waved and we were plunged suddenly back into the silent movie era, **some** of our current stars would flourish using the "new" techniques—and some would not. I do not believe in accident, and prefer to think, analyze, and work out what is needed to work in any particular time and medium.

In the Bibliography is a book called *The New Breed* where up-and-coming young actors answer questions. To me the most revealing is their answer to, "If two other actors were up for the same part as you, all three of you were equal in terms of looks, talent, etc., why should a director choose you for the part over the other two actors?" It is revealing because they all give more or less the same answer, that they have less fear and are more daring than the others. The trouble is, they all give the same answer; and one look at their pictures, at their very attractive faces and bodies, leads one to think that this may be, in fact, the real reason they are up and coming.

And an answer for all those who complain that things are now so rushed and mechanical compared with the "good old days":

My friend, the "laughing granny" Margot Stevenson, was asked to audition for Scarlett O'Hara in the great search for the right actor in 1937. At that time she was starring in a play on Broadway, but she still went to the trouble of hiring a period dress, rehearsing and practicing a wonderful piece, having a special hair-do and makeup and arriving in a hired limousine.

When she got to the studios where the tests were being made, she was asked to walk up to a mark and say her name, then look left to "see" Ashley; look right to "see" Rhett and—and that was it!

So when you next come back from an unsatisfactory experience, be thrilled that you are now part of the great tradition of auditions!

Chapter Ten

Rehearsals and Technicals

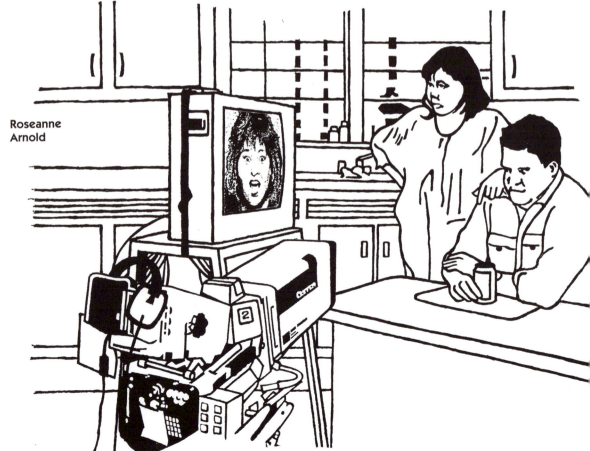

Roseanne
Arnold

REHEARSALS AND TECHNICALS

An actor I know was once called up by a casting director and told that she was wanted to play the small part of a nun. Could she travel up to Scotland from London that night? Of course, she said yes, and a page of script with a few lines for the nun arrived just before she set out for the station. The train arrived in the north, where she went straight to a hotel. Early the next morning, she was dressed as a nun, driven across wild roads and windswept moors and delivered to a field where there was a film crew. A man wandered up, vaguely greeted her and said that she was to stand on this mark, a car would drive up, and the dialogue would be delivered. As he wandered away she called after him (for he **was** the director), "You did want a Scottish accent, didn't you?" "Sure—Action!"

This is known as a short rehearsal period. Long rehearsals can take, well, much longer, involving months of research, living as your character would live and work—oh, all sorts of things. But the shorter rehearsal period is becoming more common, and it is therefore up to the actor—and his preparation—to give the best results on the screen.

If it is going to be your first ever piece of screen work, do **not** pretend you have been doing this all your life. After all, the crew will all know it is your first time, and all that energy and concentration would be better spent on learning about and observing your craft. Far better to be the known novice. It allows you to ask naive questions; it allows you to take lots of notes—and you should. How do you know which ones will be valuable? Only experience will tell. So take lots of notes until you know which are to be most valuable to you. Nothing is more irritating to a director than to block a scene or make a little comment about some business or mood and an hour later to find the actor in his excitement has forgotten it!

Multicamera Rehearsals

To rehearse a multicamera television show can be quite different from rehearsing for a movie, although there are some common elements to both.

In multicamera shoots each and every move needs to be rehearsed and plotted throughout the scene, so the delicate ballet between actors, cameras and sound can take place. With a single camera, on the other hand, you tend to rehearse each shot as it comes up. I hope you will not skip this next bit about multicamera just because you are so certain you will only be doing single camera movies.

The rehearsal starts with everyone sitting around a table for the read-through. This is the beginning of your opportunity to convince and persuade everyone that you are going to give a good **screen** performance. First rule—don't read too loud; don't read to all the others as an audience; read it as if you are being shot in close-up. I have known actors who have had to study the faces opposite them to see when the lips stop moving as the only way to know when to come in with their next speech. Second rule—start to put into your performance indications or possibilities of business or reactions that you have planned to match the thoughts and emotions of the piece. Don't wait for rehearsals—it will be too late, with your fellow actors already far, far down the road. Most newcomers are amazed how **quickly** their fellow professionals are working and committing themselves to performances. But then, the professionals have been around for a while and are probably acting the reason they got their part—their type.

In all good acting (am I actually going to lay down what I think good acting is?) it should appear that the lines said are exactly what that character wanted to say at that moment. Does this sound too trite? Then I'll put it this way: the lines should fit you like a glove, and if they don't, **and you do not have the rehearsal time to get them to fit you like a glove,** ask to change the line. Most theater actors regard this as sacrilege, and take it upon themselves to say all their lines as written. In all screen work I have been involved with, the first thing that happens is the experienced actors come up with suggestions for line changes.

You see, the writer may have had one idea in mind when writing the piece and the director another when he cast it. The writer may have written it with the accent and rhythm of a certain region in mind, and you come from another. Sometimes one of the reasons you have been cast is indeed to bring to the script your knowledge and experience of the particular role you are playing. (In the same way, it is a very good idea to get an actor who used to be a real doctor or nurse to play a doctor or a nurse; he will know all the correct procedures, and if we are lucky we can get him to teach the rest of the cast for no extra fee . . .)

Always check with the production assistant or script girl if you want to suggest a line change, and since others will need to know if the script is going to be different, do it as far in advance as possible. In particular, sound people who are waiting for a certain word as the cue to fade a microphone up or down get very testy if an actor comes up with a different one unannounced.

The scenes will then be blocked, that is, all the moves decided and given out. Don't forget that blocking is a way of getting the camera to see your face— sometimes with another face at the same time. If there is a rather free air to the blocking, you might decide that your character is rearranging flowers, while the person you are speaking to is seen over your shoulder. This would help the camera see both of you (and would also mean that you were seen in a nice big close-up). Usually, though, the blocking is worked out meticulously in advance, so you must do exactly as you are told, but it is good to understand the reason behind blocking and also good to be helpful.

In the theater, blocking moves are often given to reveal character or change of mood, and the moves are often not finalized until the actor has experimented with all sorts of combinations. In the rehearsal room for a television production, the moves are planned not only to reveal faces, but also to set up pictures that tell stories. The rehearsal room often has the positions of the walls taped to the floor, with tall poles at each corner so the director can check whether he is "shooting off," that is, to make sure that a camera will only shoot the scenery and not peek off the edge of it.

Beware of soft-spoken directors.

No, not that they are not to be trusted, it is just that when a stage director wants you to be infected with his enthusiasm, he tends to give instructions in a nice loud voice, whereas the television director, wanting the intimate approach, will be soft and quiet in his instructions and commands. The trouble is, they don't always **sound** like instructions and commands, and you can fall into the trap of thinking these are only suggestions, rather than the more precise demands of the screen.

This rehearsal period may be completed all in a day, or may extend over a longer period. The actor's job is to discover all the usual wonderful, exciting emotions and so on **within** the tight framework laid down. So watch the director, see where he stands, and start to spot the sort of shots he is planning. (Perhaps he is checking to see whether his pre-planning is actually working.) Start to **adjust your performance to the choices of shot.** If you are unsure, always assume that you are being shot in tight close-up: it is so easy to bring a voice up a bit; so hard to reduce a theatrical shout to a televisual murmur.

Next might come a technical run-through. Here the technical people in charge of cameras, lights and sound get to see the show to work out solutions to the problems they will encounter in the shoot. The problem for inexperienced actors is that here, for the first time in the rehearsals, they have an audience, and there is a danger that they will **act**. What a mistake! All that energy, all that passion and commitment, for an audience looking at camera angles and lighting possibilities, discussing how to avoid boom shadows and having no eyes for any of the performances—just the actors' positions.

The experienced performer knows what technicals are all about and uses the rehearsal to check where a shot may change and what size it may be. Since there will always be a boom shadow somewhere, the technicians must work out where to put the lights in relation to the boom so the camera does not see it. The director will usually stand wherever that shot will be taken from (to let his technicians know) and the observant actor can start to learn the shooting script and figure out the camera plan.

Roseanne Arnold has the reputation of being very demanding, but then it is her performance and her talents that the audience wants to see. She is being professional when she wants to have input into the script, the style, even the shots of her show. See her at the beginning of this chapter making sure that a sequence worked the way she wanted it to work. She uses the rehearsal period to make certain that the show is as good as she can make it—she does not sit back and hope that others will sort it all out.

Shooting script, plans and cards

The system for operating a multicamera studio to record a drama is a little like the orchestration of a piece of music. Only the conductor has the complete score; all the others have just their own bits, which if played correctly at the right time will lead to a successful performance by the whole symphony.

The individual camera person does not have a script of the drama or anything like it. He has camera cards that list numbered descriptions of shots. When he hears on his headphones that one of his shots is coming up, he gets ready for it, he shoots it and then he looks at his camera card for a description of his next shot. If the camera has to move, it will say so on the camera card, and the camera person can consult the camera plan to see exactly where his camera is due to go next.

In the control room (or gallery) a switcher (or vision mixer) switches between cameras according to the shooting script. This is the script as studied by the actors but marked up to show where there is a cut from one camera to the next. It has descriptions of each shot, including size and content, alongside each line of text. This shooting script can also contain information about where music or sound effects start and stop; where bits of scenery fly in or out; where certain flats (swingers or flippers) are brought around to stop the camera seeing off the end of a set; where furniture or fireplaces must be moved to allow a camera to get farther into a room; all these sorts of things.

This shooting script is the lifeblood of the show, it is the complete score. It was prepared, of course, by the director. (**This** was what he was doing in rehearsal so frantically; not worrying about your performance, but wondering if camera number two had time after shooting through the window to rush around to get you coming through the door.) It is usually prepared before the director meets the actors, which can explain his extreme reluctance in rehearsals to change a move, for it might mean having to change a lot of camera positions and descriptions, which would mean changing the camera cards . . .

This Bible of information tells the individual cameras what to do: the switcher when to change shot, the scenic crew when and what to move, or the sound department when the shot changes from a tight one to a wide one so they can get the boom out in time before it is seen on the wide shot. It is so useful it is not, of course, given to the actors.

Well, they might want to know the size of shot or something, and we know actors only want to know about their close-ups so we had better keep this away from them and just tell them to act. (In most studios there is a pile of these camera scripts around somewhere, and it is usually possible to snatch a look to check whether your big moment is in long shot, medium or close-up. At the very least, you can casually wander behind a camera and read the camera card to see whether it says "CU: You" or "2-s You & Him" so you can prepare yourself.)

If you are really lucky, you may be in a show that has a dress rehearsal after the technical and before the shoot.

It is more likely you will be in a show that does rehearse/record—which is exactly as it sounds. If they are really in a hurry (and, oh yes, it often happens), then they will turn the cameras onto the set and, assuming you will do exactly as you did in the rehearsal room, charge straight off into a shoot. Remember—for the screen, we rehearse and then we repeat.

Single camera television

There have been many improvements in the quality of television: stereo sound, greater use of camera mounts and moves, the Steadicam and using many more locations for shoots. In the bad old days a boom shadow could be got away with or a fluffed line obscured by putting a dog bark onto the sound track. Now that everyone has his own VCR with freeze frame, well, everything must be made to higher technical standards.

All this costs a lot, and that money has to come from somewhere. All around the world, advertisers are paying less for commercials, since there is now competition from satellite, cable and from prerecorded videos, but the money to pay for all these technical advances must come from somewhere—and do we **really** need all that time to rehearse the show?

Rehearsal times have been decreasing as the demand for more product in less time has increased. (This is another reason why typecasting is only going to get worse, for it is quicker for someone to play a type that the director/producer knows, than to create one that he does not.)

There can be a short rehearsal period, which has to be fitted around the current shoot (if it is a regular drama). A typical rehearsal would entail a quick read-through, a block of the moves and a run-through so the script assistant can time it—yes, just twenty minutes to rehearse a two-minute scene. Since the actors would not have learned their lines (and those on the current shoot might not even have thought about them), there is not much scope for more than a broad approach to the scene. Details will come later in the actual shooting period, which is the only time the actors would have memorized their scripts (we hope).

Often now in single camera dramas there is not even time for a read-through; the actor is expected to be on the set knowing his lines and is immediately put into his first setup ready for the camera. There is then a stagger-through of the moves planned by the director. This start-and-stop is purely for the camera and sound people to sort out their problems. An actor, asked to stop and then start again, should not "back up" his lines and begin from an earlier moment the way he would in theater but should pick up exactly from where he left off. You see, the camera person is memorizing the scene from picture to picture, and to go back in the scene would confuse him; after all, he looks upon this as **his** rehearsal.

Having staggered through, we hope there will be time for a run-through. **This** is when you get a chance to try out some acting, although it is often only after the first take that the director is able to zero in on your performance and is able to think about acting and acting notes.

Actors deal with this situation in different ways. There are those who come in to the shoot with their scripts covered with notes. They have tried out everything and ask rather shyly if they can just possibly change the order of the words in this speech—they have **tried** to make it work, but it just does not flow.

Then there are those who come onto the floor of the shoot, ask what scene it is, grab a script, scan it quickly, agree that they think they have got it now, and then perform it with their hands in their pockets (to avoid any continuity problems). These are the actors who also make the most fuss about how the writers never invent anything interesting for their characters to perform.

Which actor do we love the best? Which actor will we do our utmost to accommodate? If the actor shows he has done his part of the work, then we are willing to adapt our work to match his opinions.

Multicamera Film

These are rehearsed like multicamera video, but shot a little differently. See Chapter Thirteen—the Shoot for more details.

Film

Some movies assemble their actors for some form of get-together, read-through and so forth. But the trouble is that with schedules and budgets being so tight, it is often a matter of the main actor flying in just for his scenes and flying off again as soon as possible. It is no exaggeration that, within half an hour of meeting someone for the first time, you can be in bed with him shooting an intimate scene.

Actors usually grab any opportunity they can to go over their lines with each other, and if you are cast with fellow performers who like this way of working, then quite a lot can be done during the inevitable delays on a shoot. But be warned there are those who believe in spontaneity and will **not** rehearse or read with anyone until the take. We have discussed the ideal versatile actor earlier, whichever way of working seems required, **you** should be able to do that!

Being late

It is really bad to be late. It holds everyone up and makes for a negative atmosphere on the set. So don't ever be late. And if you **are** ever late, don't compound the error by coming up with a boring excuse. At the very least come up with a plausible explanation that makes us feel better—"I had to help an old lady who was knocked down at a crossing and whose wig came off"—rather than an explanation that makes us feel worse—"I overslept."

Think about it. It can be better to be interesting than to be truthful—a familiar refrain?

Secrets from the Rehearsal Room

- do not pretend it is not your first time when it is
- come in with proposed line changes where necessary
- do not read too loudly
- check from the blocking where cheating will be necessary
- learn the shot sizes, and adjust your performance accordingly
- take careful notes
- DON'T BE LATE!

Chapter Eleven

Directing Actors for the Screen

Spencer
Tracy and
Katharine
Hepburn

DIRECTING ACTORS FOR THE SCREEN

You might wonder what a chapter addressed to directors is doing here in a book for you actors?

Well, it should interest you to see what directors ought to be thinking of, and it would be nice for you to know what they are trying to achieve, so that you can help them get there more easily—**and** help yourself to be more effective.

So here we go.

DIRECTORS' NOTES

Script

When studying a scene, note which moments are confrontational and which are cooperative. As a very general rule of thumb, cross-cut between shots or cameras on confrontational moments, and try to keep a contained shot for cooperative ones.

To "bat-and-ball" (cut from one person to another on each line of alternating dialogue) in a scene where there is no conflict **creates** conflict between the intent of the scene and its style.

Note where there are changes in thought or mood in the scene, and mark these with moves or pieces of business. An actor who, in the middle of a scene, gets up and moves away or takes off her glasses is helping the audience to understand that here is a change of tack, a change of thought.

By so marking these moments, you also help the actor to remember where she is emotionally and so guide the interpretation of the scene.

Acting

Beware of eye-to-eye contact.

This may seem radical, since an alarming number of actors do not feel comfortable unless they are actually looking the other person in the eye. In many cases, this very eye contact **stops** them from performing well.

Let me explain.

When we are talking to someone, we put onto our faces and into our demeanor the "social" message that we wish to convey: our niceness, our desire to be liked, our wish to gain influence, etc. None of these would be possible if we put onto our faces exactly what we **really** felt and thought about the person we were talking to. That sickly smile as we talk to the traffic officer, wondering if we are going to get a ticket, is a good example. The honest, helpful look as we gently remove a loaded gun from the hand of a five-year-old is another. We do not radiate what we really feel; we show what we believe to be appropriate at that moment. When actors maintain eye contact, this is what they are doing—reflecting what might be deemed appropriate in a social context.

If we want to know how they **really** feel (the **subtext**), then we must look into their minds, or stage the scene in such a way that the one person **cannot see** the other's face, and so **both** actors can share with the audience how they really feel, while saying the "polite" thing.

This explains why we in screen work so often place one actor behind another, both looking the same way, something we **never** do in real life. On screen it allows us to get at the subtext of a scene. Look at the beginning of the chapter, where Katharine Hepburn is sternly addressing the back of Spencer Tracy. In a real life situation she would never stand there, but for the screen, it worked just fine, as we the audience can see both the intensity on her face and the resignation on his listening one.

Get an actor to come **toward** the camera (to get something from a foreground table or to gaze out of an invisible window, for example), and both the actor **and** the other actor(s) in the scene will present to the camera both the text **and** the subtext. The wife washing the dishes as she asks her husband over her shoulder for a divorce is shot in a manner that allows both characters to share with the audience how they feel about each other, and about the current situation.

Gazing into each others' eyes would have destroyed all that.

There are, of course, many moments when the characters **will** be looking straight at each other as you cut from one to the other. Ironically, this crosscutting can sometimes work better when they are acting with no one rather than with their partners. The following exercise might help to demonstrate this idea. I have done it often, but don't believe me—try it yourself.

Fake eyes exercise

I set out to shoot a whole series of two-handed scenes (scenes with two people in them), shooting two matching two-shots. I tell the actors that later on I shall shoot the scenes again after they have seen the rushes and noted how they did. I then play the results back to the participants.

When I do in fact repeat the exercise, I pretend that the other "actor" is unavailable, so every scene has to be recorded as a single shot. The floor manager reads the other person's lines in a monotone, and an assistant holds a piece of paper, on which is roughly drawn a pair of eyes (to give the actor the correct eyeline). It is **this** that each participant has to act with. The two actors in the scene, then, are not allowed to act with each other as in the first time they performed it, but have to do their parts of the scene separately with the stage manager reading in the lines.

Every time I do this, every actor gives a **better** performance the second time. In other words, when there is no other actor to relate to (or be distracted by?) then there is a better actual performance. Now that there is no one glaring her in the eye, the actor no longer has to do the "polite," social, "true-to-life" thing but can allow her face to show her inner thoughts—the very thing good screen acting is all about.

So an actor works better without relating to anyone else? Without getting any eye contact? Yes—it is a bit worrying, isn't it? (But there is a famous international actor who is very nearsighted and refuses to wear contact lenses on stage. This way, she says, she can react to how she thinks the other actors ought to be reacting, rather than be limited by what they actually do.)

British actor Dirk Bogarde tells a story of filming a scene in time-tight conditions, a scene in which he had a large dinner party to address. After the wide establishing shot, he told the director that for his own close-ups all the other actors could be dismissed so the movie could save on overtime. He then delivered his whole speech to the eyeline above the various chalk marks that indicated where the different guests had been sitting. Since he is a very fine screen actor, his performance was magical and, he says, easier to do than if they really had been there.

Jane Fonda had never had an easy time with her father off-screen, and the making of *On Golden Pond* was in part as real a meeting of two generations as it was in the script. In the great coming-together scene, for her close-up she asked that a light be shone on her father's face (life imitating art?) so that she could **really** act to her father's face as her character asked for understanding and forgiveness. The shot completed, the camera was turned around to shoot Henry Fonda's close-up. "Do you want me to stand in your eyeline?" she asked, anxious to give to him what she had needed for herself. "No," he replied, "I am not that kind of actor," and he proceeded to do all **his** reactions and speeches to an invisible partner.

By the way, I believe that neither was right or wrong. Each was using **whatever worked** to get the best results. (I am not so sure it did that much for father-daughter relationships, though.)

The frame

Every picture tells a story, and when you are shooting pictures, stories are being told whether you like it or not. Actors' instincts are very good about relationships and character moves, but only the very experienced understand how this relates to the actual images presented on the screen. Sometimes actors have to be where they are because the picture demands it, and your job (and their job) is to make it appear that that is what their **characters** wanted to do—but they must be in the correct place.

Here in the West our eyes scan a picture from left to right. We have done this millions of times as we read from left to right, and it carries over onto the screen. This means that our attention to the screen is not balanced, that a person on screen right will get a little bit more attention than one on screen left. You can use this to strengthen a weaker than hoped for performance (put the actor screen right) or to hide a less than effective performance (put her screen left). Movement from left to right as you look at the screen gives a smoother feeling than movement from right to left—it is not accidental that in the early Westerns it was common for the good guys to gallop from left to right, and the bad guys from right to left. (In English pantomime, a centuries-old tradition, the Fairy always appears on the left as you look at the stage, the Devil on the right.)

The shoot

Actors love to "act" (of course), but they sometimes deliver better reactions when they are relaxed and at ease than when they are "acting." I have already talked earlier in Chapter Eight—Acting about how non-real actions can convey an apparent reality (remember the sneeze?). Once for a two-character scene, Robert De Niro wanted to feel very bad to get the correct expression in his eyes, so he hit the other actor—whom he liked. This resulted in excellent acting for the screen: Robert De Niro has tears in his eyes. (What was in the eyes of the other actor, I wonder?) When Steven Spielberg wanted a look of wonderment in the little boy's eyes in *Close Encounters* he had the prop man dress up as a giant teddy bear for the boy to meet suddenly at the bottom of the stairs. For directing as for acting: whatever works.

I was once shooting a large crowd scene, and by accident the camera was recording the moments leading up to the start of the scene. During editing, this is what I saw: actors milling about, moving, looking really at ease and realistic; the first assistant shouts, "Stand by!" and the actors all settle down; the first assistant cries, "Action!"—and everyone freezes in unnatural poses. Makes you think, doesn't it: "Action!" equals freeze?

A way around this is to have a quiet word with your camera operator that she should start recording the events from just before "Action!" is called to **just after** "Cut!" is called. You will be delighted at some of the natural and imaginative reactions that you can use later in the editing sessions, sometimes for moments far removed from the time they were taken. Sometimes, they are put into entirely different scenes—but whatever works!

Single versus multicamera

We all love to shoot with a single camera, for then we can be filmic and try out all sorts of things. If we are to work in a studio with many cameras, we can still do good work, but one of the biggest dangers in shooting with more than one camera is to use too many of them. Try to stick to two for a scene whenever you can.

To explain: when two actors are talking to each other, and you are cross-shooting them with two cameras, you can light and compose shots well, because the key light for one actor becomes the back light for the other, and vice versa. The results very nearly match those you can get with one camera. The moment a third camera is used for anything more than a close-up of a prop, a twitching hand or a tapping foot, then the lighting for that third camera comes straight at the actors, ruining the lighting for the other two, and you get that "generalized" look so common with multi-camera dramas. For a fast-paced soap, of course, there is no alternative, but it is surprising how often you don't really **need** all those cameras. By rationing them and using them cunningly you can get a much higher level of achievement in your shots.

Actually, with the increasing pressure on productions to get the maximum out of a shooting day, quite a few of the single camera productions do, in fact, use two cameras when shooting static two-handed shots to speed up the

> **Directors' Secret Thoughts**
>
> • why won't actors cheat in a contained, cooperative scene when I ask them to?
>
> • why do actors always want eye-to-eye contact when it is often better without?
>
> • why do actors act better when they are acting with a blank space rather than their fellow actors?
>
> • why do some actors freeze when I shout "Action!"
>
> • why don't actors give me more when I ask for it?

process and so buy time for the more complicated pieces of shooting. As long as the actors' movements are not too extravagant, there need not be too great a compromise in camera positions and lighting.

Even in the grand world of major moviemaking, there is an increasing use of more than one camera. Here is it used during the shooting of, say, a medium close-up, so a second camera can simultaneously shoot the tight close-up. Why not, if it saves time and gives more alternatives in the editing?

Editing film versus editing video

Imagine you are setting up a cutting room (or an editing suite) for editing **film**. How much would it cost from scratch? How much if the goods were second-hand? Now you can spend those weeks or months in the film-editing suite getting the show exactly the way you want, adding a frame here, rearranging a running order there.

Now imagine setting up a **video** editing room, and you can immediately see that the cost is so huge that no company is going to give you the hours (days, even weeks) that film editing can allow you. Three days to edit three half-hour episodes—that is what you might expect to be given.

So one of the radical differences between **shooting** on film or video is the **time** allowed to edit the results. Even if you could shoot shots like those you would use in film on a single video camera, even if you had the time to put into your schedule all those fancy (no, necessary) shots you could possibly dream up, you would not have the **time** in the editing suite to put them together. This is why your shooting style will be determined by the style of your medium (and why actors need to know why you are working in one way this week with rust, and a different way next week with silver).

Casting

There are so many stories of a wonderful production being cast by accident, of the wrong person being offered a part that turned out just right, that it almost seems a mistake to be too logical about casting. I would recommend going by instinct—cast who you feel is right, not who you think is right. If by chance you are wrong, well, next time your instincts will be even better. If you cast by logic, it is much harder to get better at it, as logic and acting are not always the best of bedfellows.

I hope some of the things in this book will push you gently toward one actor rather than another. But ultimately it is you who will be working with her, and you know what the pressures and opportunities will be. Just remember that there are those actors who are wonderful in the audition room—and are never as good again.

Beware of holding a casting session just to make people happy. Do **not** call in someone when you know the part is gone, but you think it will cheer her up. (Yes, directors have been known to do this.) Actors are so keen to work, so anxious not to miss an opportunity, that they will cancel work (and lose money) for the day, go for an expensive hairdo, hire a cab—in other words spend precious time and money to turn up for what you were considering a favor to them. If they ever find out, they will not thank you.

In the Fall of 1993 I was asked to do a Block Shoot for *Brookside*, where I had to shoot 30 scenes from 14 different episodes for the next four months in just three shooting days. (It all had to do with clearing an actor from the series, and with getting full value from an expensive set.) Jokingly, I told them that they only hired me to do it because I was very quick. "No," was the disconcerting reply, "It is because you are nice—and quick!" Nice and quick—the modern criteria. What an epitaph.

Chapter Twelve

Announcers
(and the Art of
Being Interviewed)

Oprah
Winfrey

ANNOUNCERS (AND THE ART OF BEING INTERVIEWED)

The techniques and ideas dealt with up to now also work extremely well for announcers, as well as lecturers, newscasters, weather people, interviewees—even people stopped in the street by a news crew and asked for their opinions.

The same liturgy comes up:

- React before you speak.
- Project to the microphone only.
- Give extra animation when speaking at low levels.
- Happily present **yourself**.

The first three elements are easy to grasp and to practice—but happily present yourself? Here's how.

I was working with some businessmen on how to present themselves better for the inhouse videos their company sends out. First I had them bring in their official "company" photo along with their favorite snapshot.

Then I had them give a short speech in the manner of their official photo. We repeated the exercise using the "favorite" snapshot, getting them to match their manner to **that**. All of them came across better during the second exercise. That is Oprah opposite, showing her bubbly personality both in a snapshot, and of course in the magic way she comes across on screen.

Once I was working one-on-one with a managing director who had come dressed in a rather tight double-breasted suit. Newly appointed, he wanted to make a video to be shown to all his employees, but when he made his presentation to the camera, he was stilted and stiff, not the image he wanted to project to his workforce.

I could see immediately what the problem was: he was ashamed of his waistline and was trying to hide it. Shock tactics sometimes work best. "Now do the speech again," I told him, "but this time with your jacket off. All I want you to concentrate on is showing to the audience what a wonderful, big, fat gut you've got." (Yes, I put it just like that!)

Well, he did—and the result was a wonderful, warm, witty and effective speech. Having been forced to face up to his greatest fear, he wasn't spending any time fighting it, and this allowed his natural charm and intelligence to come through.

Do you think you have the nerve to present to the world your greatest secret fear? By doing so, you can release all that negative energy and channel it positively into presenting a nice talk, lecture or interview.

Try the store window test.

Imagine you are walking down the street, and you look into a store window, but you are not actually looking at anything in the window, you are looking at your own reflection. Quick: **which bit of you are you looking at?** You will find that it is usually the bit you wish was not the way it is (the big rear end, the balding head, the straggly hair, the stooped shoulders). This demonstrates what you need to face up to and boldly flaunt, rather than hide from.

I tried this test out with a group of professional actors in New York, and one admitted that she always looked at what she thought was her large rear (although the rest of her is quite, quite beautiful). Discussing this, she suddenly announced that all the mirrors in her home were half-length, only showing her from the waist up. My advice was to get a full-length one and to get to know **and love** the way she was. I even got her to act a piece while "showing off the rear." It did not show, of course, but her **performance** was so much more relaxed, convincing and powerful.

Present yourself and your personality, and if in doubt, make sure that the relaxed and happy you we meet off-camera is the same person we meet on camera. So, actors and announcers alike, do not fall into the trap of being more interesting in the canteen than on the screen. Concentrate on that Audience of One (the camera), and give it those conspiratorial glances and asides, just the way you do at business meetings, planning meetings and the like.

Technical points of view

The more you understand about the work and the problems of others, the better your contribution will be to the program.

Another personal anecdote: I was taking part in a documentary on aspects of television and was in a group of four having an unscripted conversation, supposedly over lunch. I could see that the director was going to have great trouble cutting the show together, because there were no linking shots. At the end of the group shot, he took some quick cutaways of each of our faces, so in mine I did a great deal of "eating" as I looked left, looked right, quickly flashed my eyes left again, and so on.

When the program was shown, my friends laughed because it seemed to be mostly about me eating salad. Whenever the director wanted to cut from one face to another, he would cut to my face to get him there, and this led to a lot of my face on the screen.

No, I was not smugly trying to be seen more, I **was** giving the director what I knew would be needed in the editing suite. (But it **did** get me more screen time.)

The bit about "provide a motivation for all camera moves" from Chapter Four—the Camera also applies to interviews and presentations, and particularly to the TelePrompTer or autocue. The audience at home must believe that the one thing you **want** to do is to be reading those words at precisely that angle, at that height and in that manner. When it goes wrong, it must be **exactly** the moment that you **wanted** to look down at the script on the table and read it from there.

This "make us think you want to" or "motivation" is not so easy at first, but as long as you know that it is your long term goal, then you can start moving toward it from your very first screen appearance.

Announcers especially suffer from the "frozen butterfly" look, when as a result of the camera being turned on you, you seem to be riveted to the back of the chair, head clamped upright and generally stiffened up.

Just because you are sitting in a chair does not mean that you cannot move. Oh, I know that you should not move much from left to right, otherwise you might fall out of the frame. But you **can** move backwards and forwards. In fact you can see newscasters doing this often: " . . . and the baby elephant was happily reunited with its mother"—leaning forward as a serious expression comes over the face—"In the middle east today . . . " (We know it is going to be bad news.) Again, watch the experienced ones, noting exactly what they do, not what you thought they did.

Interviews

In an interview situation, try to put yourself in the director's seat, and ask yourself, "What does he want to see?" The short answer is "good television," and **that** is more often a funny look, reaction or grimace than a witty phrase or statement. Read Chapter Nine—Auditions for confirmation that when you are being interviewed, you should work just as hard at listening as when you are speaking.

It is so embarrassing (and ineffective for your contribution) if, when you are introduced to the audience, you sit there like an embarrassed prune. **Do** something—be discovered looking down, look up after your name is mentioned, smile shyly into the camera as if to say, "There you are" to a well-loved friend (the audience behind the lens). Then look toward the introducer, smile at any witticism he makes, shake your head in wonderment at the nice things being said about you (or shake your head in sorrow at the lies they are telling about you). In other words, **actively** start being effective.

When you are asked questions, do not reply to the questioner, but to where the questioner **would** be sitting if they were as close as your microphone. Since you are most likely to be rigged up with a radio mike, that is very close indeed. Be careful not to become dreamy and slow as you excitedly and enthusiastically go through your routine **with low vocal levels**. Well, it **is** a routine, isn't it?

If you are trying to get a particular point across, and you suspect that the questioner is speaking to a different agenda, use the John Wayne technique. He had a habit of having a rising inflection at the end of a thought. On one of those talk shows he was asked why he did so. "Easy," he replied, "If I had a downward inflection, then the camera can cut away from my face. But if I have a rising inflection, then I haven't finished yet, and the camera cannot cut away, and I get a longer shot of my face." He was a very skilled screen actor indeed.

Try it now. See how long you can go on speaking without ever dropping your voice.

What? You are starting to sound like a television evangelist? Well, why do you think **they** do it? It keeps the attention and becomes mesmerizing. Go on, do a speech again **in the manner of a television evangelist.** Effective, isn't it?

Chapter Thirteen

The Shoot

Goldie
Hawn

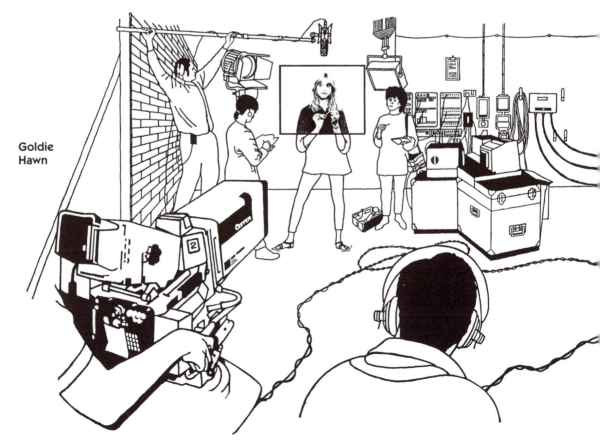

THE SHOOT

This is it: the moment of truth. This is where the preparation and work of all contributors is finally put to the test. Unlike theater, you cannot hope to get it right tomorrow if today is not up to scratch. You have to be perfect—**now**.

There are many pitfalls that can prevent you from being at your best, the first being the fact of the shoot itself. There is no gradual build up. You suddenly find yourself in the middle of bright lights, bustling people and menacing equipment, and you are expected to be tender, vulnerable, emotional and sincere. No wonder so many inexperienced actors find the pressure so intense that they retreat into safety, into the sort of acting they have done before and which has brought them this far: theater acting.

It is so difficult to learn from your more experienced acting partners or from the experts you may encounter because you just can't see what they are up to. (Remember Laurence Olivier and Marilyn Monroe? If **he** couldn't see what she was doing, what chance have you?) Look at Goldie Hawn on the opposite page. **Now** can you appreciate what sort of skills and talents are needed to come across as simple and sincere in the middle of all that chaos?

The shoot can bring out the worst in actors: Their voices can get louder (but where is the microphone?), their gestures more expansive (but what size shot is it?), and their movements more flowing (but what mark must they hit?). Don't forget—in the theater we rehearse, and then we perform. For the screen we rehearse (if we are lucky), and then we **repeat**.

Multicamera shoots—video

The shoot is a continuation of the process already described. (See Chapter Ten—Rehearsals and Technicals.) Things happen very quickly, with instructions usually channeled (and sometimes retranslated) through the first assistant/floor manager. If the cameras cannot see you according to the pre-planned camera script, then it is likely that **you** will be moved rather than a camera. (Moving you is easy; moving a camera may affect many other people).

When a scene is shot, the director has just a few seconds to decide if: (a) it is all acceptable and she can move on to the next scene; (b) it was not acceptable and she must repeat the scene just done; or (c) one or two shots of the scene need to be repeated, and just those will be done. It is always a good idea for you to quietly tell the floor manager if you feel you could do it all better. The director may feel you were just fine, or she may add your concern to her own and decide to do the whole thing all over.

In the middle of a scene, do not stop—unless you are about to be seriously injured. Don't stop—even when everything seems to have gone wrong.

Let me tell you a story. I was shooting a multicamera drama and got to my last three-minute scene with twenty minutes to spare. (Here I should add that I was working at the BBC, and when your time is up, that is it—they turn the plugs off!) I relaxed a little as we got ready for the last scene which was set in a pub. I did not worry when first a light fell over, then a camera went on the blink, and then . . . And **then** it was five minutes to the end of recording time, and I realized that we would have to get the scene first time, since there was no time to do it twice.

The scene was going nicely, the actors were acting, the smoke machine adding that haze that looks so nice in a pub setting, and the main character went off to get cigarettes and returned to his friends. We reached the last page of dialogue, cutting between nice close-ups on screen, when one of the friends (actually, a friend of mine—correction, a **former** friend of mine) stopped acting. "Sorry Patrick, we have to stop; his cigarette is on fire." And yes, it was indeed burning the way a cigarette shouldn't, but the point is, **it was not visible on screen!** By the time we had sorted it out, the deadline had been reached, the machines turned off. My producer had to negotiate with the unions for extra time which was reluctantly granted; my show therefore cost several thousand pounds more than it should. If my "friend" had just kept on acting, all would have been fine. As it was, that producer has never reemployed me, and, no, I have not reemployed my friend. You see, **his** perception of what was going on was not the same as ours in the control room. Never stop acting—please!

Another one:

For the final image of an episode, I very much wanted a rising crane shot of the nurse-heroine walking down her hospital ward. My producer told me I could not afford the crane, so I had to abandon the idea. In the middle of the shoot, the technical director told me that they could rig a camera up onto a lighting hoist and get the shot that way. So we rushed and rushed, finished the show with five minutes to spare, got the camera rigged, rolled tape and asked the heroine to walk. As she did, we started the lighting hoist—and she stopped walking. She stopped because she did not expect a noise (it was the noise of the hoist), and she thought something had gone wrong. By the time it was explained to her, time had run out, the cameras had been switched off, and she had lost her shot—because she had stopped acting before hearing the magical word "Cut."

In case you think I am the know-it-all who gets it all right, here is a story against myself. During my BBC television training I was trailing a production, that is, following an episode of a prestigious drama from rehearsals through to the studio. One particular scene was done, and it was very bad. There were boom shadows, several shots were out of focus, and one of the actors fluffed a line. "That's fine," said the director, "Let's move on to the next scene." Well, I just **knew** that all was not well, so I thought the director would like me to speak up and point out the errors. "Shut up!" was his reply to my starting to tell him, "But there was . . ." He eventually silenced me, and he **did** go on to the next scene, angrily waving me to go away. Later, after the shoot when he had cooled down, he explained the situation to me. One of the guest artists had only agreed to be in the show because she had two scenes, but unfortunately the show was running over, and the first scene was to be cut. He did not want to tell her, "Your first scene is cut. Now let's do the second one," so he decided to do the first scene any which way and then move on. He did **not** want my voice piping up (and being heard all over the studio on the headphones that relay to all wearers—the cameras, sound, assistants, electricians—all the conversations that go on in the control room) saying how that scene was unacceptable. You see, I did not know the full story, and had made an assumption that was **not helpful to the shoot.** Leave the drastic decisions to the decision makers.

In the shoot, the operative camera is the camera with a little red light on it. Although you should not wait for the light to come on before you act, it is certainly information that you can put to good use in a shoot. Imagine, for example, that you are facing another character, and you know that there are three cameras on the scene: one over her shoulder looking at you; one over your shoulder looking at her; one out to the side getting a two-shot of the both of you. Well, if you can see the red light **ahead** on the camera, you know

156

What a bad
three-shot
looks like
on screen. . .

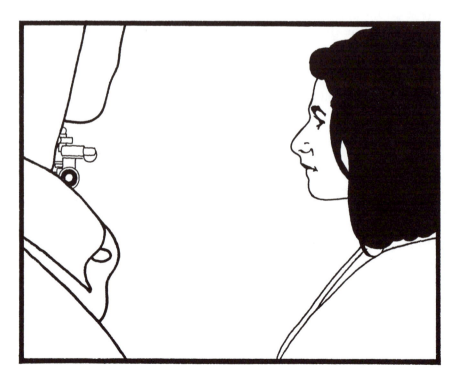

. . . and
what the
actor sees
of the
camera

What a good three-shot looks like on screen. . .

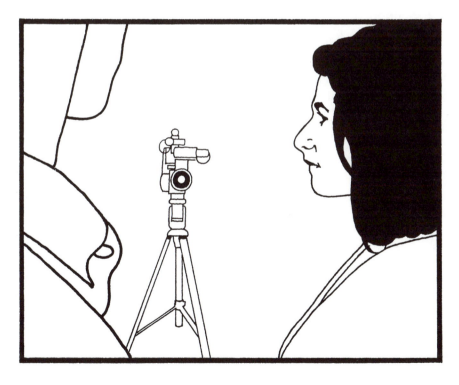

. . . and what the actor sees of the camera

it is a tight shot of you (so you can do some good facial reactions). If you glimpse the red light out of the corner of your eye, you know it is the camera to the side with a wide two-shot (and so you can put in some good character revealing gestures). If you can't see a red light at all then that means that the shot must be coming over your shoulder to your fellow actor, so you know not to waggle your head into her shot.

The simple geometry used in shooting can teach you where the cameras will be, and how to guess what the shot is. When you act, part of your brain deals with the acting side and another part of your brain must function as your own private technical director, keeping tabs on where the cameras and microphones are, and noting and remembering which marks have to be hit.

Speaking of marks, the most useful actors are those who can hit their marks and find the camera. Although this applies to both single and multicamera shoots, I am putting it here, since finding the camera is much more necessary in a fast-moving multicamera shoot.

On page 156 is a picture of a bad three-shot, along with what the actor involved would see. This is followed on page 157 by a picture of a good three-shot, with the point of view of the same actor.

As I have mentioned before, one of the problems with working on a shoot is that, unlike the theater, practically no one on the technical end has actually worked in front of a camera. So what is perfectly obvious to them, can be all too obscure to you. As an example, looking at the first example of a bad three-shot, it is so crystal clear to all the co-workers—the director, the switcher, the camera people, the sound people—exactly **where** the actor should be standing, that they can't understand that it is not at all clear to the actor. If you make sure that you see the **camera lens** exactly in the middle of the gap between your two fellow actors, then you will be correctly placed in the three-shot. (It is the same point of view as properly cheating yourself around, as in Chapter Four—the Camera.)

To act brilliantly, but to miss your mark and so put your face partially behind someone else, means that we cannot use the material at all. To act in a so-so manner, but to be in the correct place at all times, means that we can use the material. In other words, it is often more important to be in the right place than to act well, for your best acting moment can be rejected if you are one inch off your mark.

This upsets some actors, who know that a change of a move or gesture means a change of thought, but you must remember that a director can say to the camera operator, "Move the camera left," and it moves; to the boom operator, "Raise the boom," and it moves. When she says to the actor, "Move a little right," she does not want to hear, "What's my motivation?" I am afraid that there will be a tendency to treat you like all the other elements on the set, something to be moved and adjusted minutely and at will to suit the framed picture. As long as you understand this, you can contribute to the shoot as a co-worker, and not play actor-as-victim.

Be aware that as a scene progresses and the tension rises, it is more than likely that the shots will get closer; so your vocal level should be adjusted down. It is a very strange experience, building a speech emotionally, but getting quieter as you do it. Remind yourself of this from Chapter Six—Sound and Vocal Levels.

Multicamera shoots—film

These shoots are most particular to some Hollywood situation comedies, where the cameras waltz around the studio to meet actors who have rehearsed moving around a rehearsal room. Instead of video cameras all connected up to a control room, however, there are four film cameras all shooting simultaneously. (This means that everything is recorded all the time, not just the stuff seen by the camera with the red light.)

The director stands on the floor looking at a monitor with four video pictures on it—the output from the four cameras. The advantage of this is that if anything goes wrong, it can be put right immediately. The disadvantage is that no one can be **sure** which shot is going to be used and so cannot be sure what size of shot to act for.

I was watching the making of one such comedy in Los Angeles recently. The director was a courteous gentleman ("Action, please!"), and the actors were superb. There was a large office in the set's background, full of bit part actors doing wonderfully directed detailed business. When the director called out for a line to be repeated (because the actor had just spoken through a laugh by the audience), all the background artists quietly backtracked two or three steps, ready to be in the correct position for the repeated line.

Good, good screen acting.

Multicamera Shoot Secrets
• don't stop
• be aware of the red light on the front of a camera
• hit your marks—and hit the deep three-shots
• build your emotions as you decrease the volume
• particularly with a studio audience, don't speak louder than the Star

Perhaps I should talk here of what to do with audience reactions. The main thing is, do **not** pitch your performance to them—and there will be a tremendous temptation for you to do so. That whole, lovely audience is sitting out there just waiting to receive your finely-honed performance, but you must never forget: **it is only an Audience of One.** Look closely at the people in the audience, and you will see that they do not watch the actors on the floor. They watch the nearest television monitor and listen to the sound as it comes over the loudspeakers. So you perform for the cameras, as usual, and use the audience reactions to give you **timing** for the laughs.

And because the energy level for a comedy is higher than for, say, a heavy drama, you can use the simplest of my rules: **never speak louder than the Star.** After all, the regulars in the show will have evolved a style and format that fits the show, and the audience, both in the studio and at home, will assume that whatever the stars do is correct. Base your performance on **that** level.

Single camera shoots

In the theater, we rehearse and then we perform.
On the screen, we rehearse and then we repeat.

On a shoot, your relationship to the work is very different from that of the other workers. For a start, they have all been working together on this shoot, usually in advance of any meeting with you, and so the camaraderie that theater engenders has already been created—between the director and the technicians.

Your scene is very important to you (of course), but you don't have a complete picture of all that is going on and cannot judge just how it fits in—whether it really is a scene that must have time spent on it, or whether it is one of those "bread and butter" moments that, frankly, are to be got through as efficiently and speedily as possible.

Single Camera Shoot Secrets

- remember your Audience of One
- rehearse—then **repeat**
- remember you are part of a complex team, and learn to cooperate
- keep your eyelines during lineup
- plan and rehearse your continuity

Your call has probably meant that you have been waiting around for quite some time before you are used. The director and crew will have been hard at it from dawn. You don't know what excitements they may have been through. Maybe they have been kept waiting by equipment breaking down, or the weather playing dirty tricks on them, or even of an actor not delivering either lines or a performance. So to complain about being kept waiting is, to put it very mildly, not a sensible attitude to have. The context, you see, is totally different for the crew than for the cast.

As you know (from all the other books on screen acting you have read?), things are not shot in any order that makes sense to you. **Learn** what that sense is, and try to understand why we work the way we do. This will enable you to contribute to the shoot better, rather than getting indignant and upset by imagined slurs or supposed incompetence.

It is so costly to shoot, that the producers more or less try to keep the camera and all the associated equipment working all the time. This means that not only do they try to shoot all the scenes together that occur in one set or location, but they try to shoot **everything** in the same direction as well. After all, it can take a long time to move all the lights around from looking in one direction to looking in the opposite direction, and time spent moving lights is time not spent working with cameras and microphones and actors to get good results on to the screen. (Did you notice that actors were not put at the head of that list?)

If you have a costume or makeup change, that will take time too, so the shoot schedule is arranged so that, where possible, all changes take place at a time when the crew can keep working. The eventual shoot schedule, hopefully carefully worked out, may seem lunatic to you, but it would look quite good to a production manager who has to keep the director and the crew working in such a way as to get the job done on time, on budget.

Time (literally seconds) secrets

I have sometimes noticed an actor, on the way over to the location or set where we are waiting for her, stop for a brief word with someone. Oh, maybe it is only ten seconds wasted.

At the end of the shoot day, when your production manager tells you that you **have** to stop shooting in one minute, and you have this **two**-minute shot that you just **long** to do again, you think back and add up all those lost ten seconds when actors (or electricians, or makeup, or cameras) took an unnecessary extra few seconds all through the day, and you think dark thoughts about them all.

So—don't **you** be a second-eater-upper!

Practicalities

As each shot is set up individually, the actor is able to see and sense exactly what is required for each shot. Each time the camera is moved to a different position, or is shooting a section of a scene in a different size shot, it is called a setup. You can expect to go through anything from fifteen to forty setups in a day, depending on the complexity of the shot, whether it is outdoors or in a studio, and so on.

Sometimes the actors are taken through the scene first—they can even initiate moves in certain circumstances—then the lighting and camera people descend to work out where to put the camera and how to light the actors in the positions they are now in. For other shoots the whole sequence is carefully prepared, so that the actors are only called when the cameras and lights are ready, and then they go into a rehearsal. During the rehearsal a lot of activity can still be taking place, as the lighting crew adjusts the lights, the design crew finishes dressing the set, the prop crew sets all the action properties, and the sound crew works out how to get the microphones in the right place at the right time to get good clean sound.

If this is a shoot with stars, then their stand-ins will be doing the job of standing in the right place for the lighting crew while they line up the shot. The reason for this is simple. A shoot can be a very exhausting time, and we all want the stars to be at their best for the actual moment of shooting and not to waste their energies during the line-up period. Of course, if you are not a star, then you will be required to stand around, but don't let this distract you from your ultimate job of being excellent for the camera when the shot is taken. Keep your eyelines during the lineup. (That is, look in the directions you will be looking: one of the things they are checking is that you are correctly lit, and in particular that your eyes are properly lit— and you want that, don't you?) Remember this rehearsal is as much for the crew as it is for you. Each department must be confident that their part of the job is ready at the magical moment of a take. It may just be a simple head-and-shoulders of one character talking to another; it may be much, much more than that.

When Alfred Hitchcock was making *Stage Fright,* he had a sequence that was all one continuous shot, running for two minutes and forty seconds. It took him two and a half days to rehearse and shoot it. Why did it take him so long? If you ever get a chance to see it, you will understand why. In this shot, all in one room, Richard Todd and Marlene Dietrich move from place to place: She has to hit eight different marks; he has to hit eleven different marks; the camera moves to eleven different marks; and there are at least seventeen different points of focus that the camera has to find. During this sequence, furniture had to be put in then taken out again, lights had to fly in and be fired up, then dimmed and flown out again before the camera could swing around to see them. A complicated ballet of all the technical elements of film had to take place to get this shot looking just right. There was even one moment in the middle of the sequence when Todd walked over to Dietrich and shadowed her face; immediately, he leaned back and took his shadow off her face. In the middle of all that complexity, of saying all those lines and hitting all those marks, the actor was aware enough of the technical elements to avoid making everyone go through the whole thing yet again.

You might ask why Hitchcock did it this way, why not break up the scene into little bits the way other directors do and film all those? He was creating huge problems for all the technicians and actors, but it **was** for a good reason. This sequence is part of the famous "lying" flashback that some criticized Hitchcock for: as Richard Todd's character is telling his girlfriend what had just happened, there is a flashback of his explanation, but by the end of the film, we discover that it was all a lie—the flashback is **not** what really happened. I think that the genius of Hitchcock is that he shot this sequence in this complicated, almost ostentatiously difficult way as a subtle way of saying to the audience that it was, in fact, a lie. We can debate the decision, but the result meant that the actors had to perform in a certain way to achieve the results—screen acting of the highest level.

Any particular setup may be repeated a number of times, and each is called a different **take**. Some actors give their best performances on the first take, some on a much later take; some directors do not like going for more than a handful of takes, some go on and on. There is no regular pattern. Sometimes the actor is given different acting notes for each take, sometimes no notes are given at all. The actor will however be expected to repeat the same moves and bits of business, and this opens up the world of continuity.

It always surprises technicians that an actor can pick up a spoon with one hand, and a few moments later when repeating the scene, pick it up with the other. Film books are full of examples of continuity mistakes: it is easy to criticize from the sidelines, but much harder to cope with in reality. Sometimes an actor will do exactly what she is told, even matching the Polaroid that was taken of a previous moment, and the continuity will **still** be wrong. It is not always the actor's fault. Try to protect yourself against mistakes, and try to prevent that most dreaded of all things—a continuity girl giving you a long list of continuity notes. The way to avoid this is to arrive on the set with all your continuity already worked out and part of you; it should be as much part of your performance as your lines, so that whatever thought is thrown at you on a set, you can devote your talent to playing the part, instead of trying to remember continuity details.

Shooting tricks

- When you are given some instructions, repeat them back to the giver. Don't say "Eh?" or "Can you repeat that?" It is even worse if you don't understand an instruction but don't say anything—and then get it wrong in the shoot. When you repeat an instruction, it provides the note giver an opportunity to confirm that you have understood, and it gives you the confidence that these rather odd instructions are **really** what you need to do.

- It is so important to hit your marks that you must develop a sense of where they are without looking down. Practice so you know how many steps it is to the mark, or work out your position in relation to the furniture, or line up two distant objects (a lamp, an exit sign) so that when they are in line you are on your mark.

- Cheat your face around to the camera by placing any property in the **camera** side hand. This means that when you look at the book, drink the drink, examine the rings or lift the pencil, all these actions will bring your face more around to camera than it was.

  In the same way, when talking to another actor, talk to her **camera side** eye, or even her ear, with your **off camera** side eye—in order to bring your own face around more to the camera.

- Always have some expression on your face at the end of a shot. **Always** think through some extra business or line that your character would do **just after the word "Cut" is shouted**. This will keep your face alive and alert right until the end (and can sometimes lead to **your** face getting the last shot of a sequence, since some of the others' faces will have turned off). One trick I have learned is to ask an actor to end a scene by vigorously exhaling (the "*Brookside* Blow Out"). It doesn't actually mean anything, but it keeps your face alive while they are cross-fading to another scene.

- Always ease yourself into the correct shot by putting weight on one leg or the other, and be ready to change weight immediately if you are not correctly positioned for the camera. Take a manic joy in being in the right place even if you have had to move, because all the other actors have missed their marks, but you **still** get into a good three-shot.

- When moving, talk fast but move slow. When walking along with the camera tracking you, lift your knees to give you the animation of walking while you are actually moving through space rather slowly. Do not let slow movements slow down your speech.

- If you need a cue to speak (because the other actor is so far away or speaking so intimately that you cannot hear her), be bold and ask for one. The crew would much rather give you a cue than not have you speak at the proper time.

- In a similar way, if you are really having problems with your lines, ask for a few of them to be placed in appropriate places, or even have them written up on boards for you to know they are there. You will have the confidence to act without having to spend too much energy trying to remember the lines. Oh, I know that it is your job to remember your lines (and because a shoot can be so complicated, you need to know your lines **really well** to cope with whatever instructions you are given just before you are about to act), but we would rather put up idiot cards for you than have endless takes ruined by you forgetting your lines.

- Assume that no note means you are doing fine. Just as I do not shout out "Good boom" after a take when the microphone was not seen, I do not necessarily give approval to any other member of the team who got everything right. To assume that silence means that everyone hates you leads to a life of paranoia.

- I have read in a book on film acting, "Don't blink." This has led to a lot of watery-eyed actors all over the world. It is right—and it is wrong. **If you have fair eyelashes**, when you blink it looks a little odd. So if you have fair eyelashes then, yes, don't blink. If on the other hand you have nice, thick, dark lashes that can flutter away to tremendous effect, then do just that. This is all part of the idea that you should do **whatever your face does best**. If you have very small eyes, then maybe you should use them a lot; very large eyes should be used with care, and so on. Develop your own personal vocabulary of what works for you.

I do not recommend the following tricks, but I have seen them used, and they do give an indication of the sort of things that can happen on a shoot.

There was an actor being filmed in a long shot. He thought it should be a much closer shot but the director wanted the long shot, so that was what was done. The only thing was, the actor never remembered his lines properly in the long shot—they only came to him perfectly when he was being filmed in close-up. Funny thing, memory.

Another time, I heard an actor mention that he thought the two-shot he was in would be better as a single on him. The director thought otherwise, so they set up the two-shot. Only the actor spoke so softly, even when asked to speak up, that the only way to get proper sound was to bring the microphone really close to him. Since this meant that the camera could see it, the only way to get rid of the microphone was to tighten the shot. The actor ended up with his single shot after all. What a strange series of events.

Conclusions

I think it takes a lot of talent to come across as ordinary.

If you come across very well, with good, believable acting full of emotion and passion, and you hit all your marks and always project to where the microphone is, I think that takes extraordinary talent.

We sometimes disparage good actors, precisely because of their skill at making a difficult, technical sequence appear easy and ordinary. "Well, I could have done as well as that," we confidently claim, not understanding quite how difficult it is. You, having read this far, will now know that you cannot just walk into a shoot straight off the street and achieve instant overnight success. It takes work, hard work, and this book is showing you just what sort of work you need to do.

There, take a look again at the beginning of this chapter, and the seemingly calm Goldie Hawn surrounded by all that chaos and elements of a shoot. Never forget when you see a nice quiet moment like this on the screen, that just outside the frame is a different world of people and equipment—and appreciate the talent and skill needed to act serenely in these circumstances.

Things that I hate that actors do on a shoot

1. Actors who stop acting before the floor manager or the director shouts "Cut!"

2. Actors who vary what they do from take to take, and don't remember what they did when the camera is moved to shoot the "reverses."

3. Actors who want to be "real," and so will not properly cheat their faces around to the camera.

4. Actors who (unannounced) change things "because it feels wrong."

5. Actors who just do not understand (or have never taken the trouble to understand) the craft of the job they are undertaking—acting on screen.

Things that I love that actors do on a shoot

1. Actors who come to the shoot with all their business planned and rehearsed and who know their lines very well.

2. Actors who add extra ideas and business to the shoot, understanding what is possible and what is not.

3. Actors who do the same business on the same syllable of a speech in every take.

4. Actors who automatically ease themselves into the right position so that they fill the screen, their two-shot is maintained, or they come to a perfect deep three-shot.

5. Actors who understand the craft of screen acting and make additions and suggestions within the framework of what is possible both technically **and** in the time available.

Chapter Fourteen

The Editor and Editing

Bette
Davis

THE EDITOR AND EDITING

General

The most common experience a director has in the editing stage is staring at the screen and wondering why he did not **insist** that the actors do more. There it is again—more, rather than less.

It does not matter what the writer intended or the director planned; in the editing, the editor is only dealing with what is **there**. The raw material he uses is no more and no less than what the camera recorded—and what the actors put into the lens.

Reactions

I know I have gone on about reactions before in Chapter Five—Reactions and Business. Now, here is another way of looking at them.

When two people are talking to each other, it is often filmed by putting the camera on one of them and recording all that he says as well as the moments in between when he listens. The camera is then pointed at the other actor, and the process is repeated. In the editing, the editor does **not** just put the person who is talking on the screen; it is **not** talking heads that we are after.

The editor will often start off on one person, and then look at the shot of the other person listening, to see if there is anything of interest going on. Frequently—especially with inexperienced actors—not a lot is, in fact, happening. I have watched in horror as a three minute take went by in the editing room all on one actor's face, and he did not do **anything** except say his one line.

We must start again with what **is** real and what **appears** to be real. In real life, if you are listening to another person speaking, you tend to put on a "polite" expression; you certainly do **not** allow your face to reflect everything you are thinking as that person is speaking. You do **not** let large expressions flow across your face, for that is a social "signal" that you wish to speak, that you wish to interrupt the conversation with some comment of your own.

On stage, if you were to react clearly and largely during another person's speech, then you would be rightly accused of "upstaging" and would be given a bad time in the dressing room afterwards.

In other words, it is "unreal" to react while another person is speaking; it is "real" for your face to react only a little. But it is also boring and unusable if you put **that** onto the screen.

When an editor/director is cutting from someone speaking to the person listening, he often only wants to take a second or so of the listening shot to liven up the talking shot.

As I described before, one can scan **reams** of listening before finding something that is usable. (Yes! **There** is something. Oh, he was only blinking.) Now, if the actor did three different reactions in a row, it would **feel** most peculiar. If it were shown to an audience, it would also **look** very peculiar. But the editor is **not** going to use **all** the reactions: he is just looking for a snippet, a "nice reaction," and if you present several, it makes you a more useful actor, doesn't it? You will **feel** peculiar doing it, but you will be presenting the editor with choices and allowing the artistic process of editing, shaping performances in the editing room, to progress with plenty of good raw material.

I was once shooting a scene between a husband and wife, where the wife had all the talking—the husband listened throughout and had just one line. By the time I got to the scene I was running late, so I shot the close-up of her first, getting all her lines down. I then turned the camera on the husband and shot what was mostly him listening. It was really boring, so seeing that I had just a minute and a half before the compulsory wrap, I asked (actually, I probably shrieked) for the camera to keep turning, rushed up to the actor and begged and implored him to let all sorts of emotions and feelings cascade across his face. I promised faithfully that I would not use anything that appeared unnatural or untrue. We then shot his reaction shots for one last time before the end of the shoot.

His face **still** showed practically nothing, so, walking away from the shoot and finding myself alongside the actor, I gently asked him why he had not done what I had asked him to do. "Well, Patrick, I **wanted** to," he replied anxiously, "But it felt like I was just pulling faces."

Yes? There was no reply I could give him, and in the editing we played the whole scene on the wife's face, for there was nothing I could cut to that added to or advanced the story. (You see, directors are not as powerful as some actors would make us out to be.) If only he had "pulled" just one face, maybe that would have been all the editor needed to cut to his face briefly and so help the audience understand what his character was feeling as his screen wife went on and on.

"Secrets"

When the screen is showing only you, and it is watched by an audience, they have this belief that only **they** can see what you are going through. If your face expresses how you really feel, the audience will believe that they are being "told" a secret, a secret that the other character cannot see.

I was recently directing a scene where a wife had to indicate to her husband that she did **not** want to be invited next door for a cup of tea. I suggested that she give a little "no" shake of her head toward her husband. "I could not do that—the next door neighbor would see it," she anxiously told me. But for this moment she was being filmed in close-up, and I reassured her that although **in real life** the neighbor could see her negative reaction, when it was on the screen, the audience would believe that only her husband would be let in on her "true" feelings.

She did it—very reluctantly—and when cut together it worked very well. It showed again how unwise it is to trust your feelings until you are experienced enough to know what "true" feelings are as defined by the camera.

Eye flashes

When you are in a scene with anybody else (but particularly three or more), the editor likes to cut from face to face with motivating moments, and one of the easiest of these is when one character flashes a glance at another.

By doing these flashes, you help the editor (and, incidentally, get your face onto the screen more often as the editor uses your face to "bounce" from one face to another). No, it is not just a selfish thing, but a practical one; I worked with an actor who had the habit of looking **away** from the other person she was speaking to, especially at the beginning of a speech. This meant that when the shots were edited together, you often forgot where the person she was speaking to was, and it all got very confusing.

Continuity

It is, of course, in editing that the effects of good and bad continuity become apparent.

It is a truism to say that your moves, and in particular your bits of business (drinking from a glass; turning the page of a book), should be at the same **precise** point in a speech when it is shot from different angles.

It always astounds screen people (but not stage people!) that an actor can act a speech one way and then a few minutes later do the same speech with the pieces of business in different places. (Part of this is that an actor always wants to improve things and so regards the shooting as a continuous process. This naturally works well on the stage but can be a drawback in screen work.)

Now there are many people who should (and do) remind the actor of his continuity—the continuity girl (or script girl), the production assistant if there is one, the camera operator, the director. It is, however, no consolation to you that it is someone else's fault if you have such differing continuity that the editor cannot cut to your best moments.

We all want the best, and the editor wants to put on screen the best moments that he sees in the rushes. It is always sad when we cannot use them, because, in the two matching shots, the moves (or angle of head or angle of shoulders) are such that we cannot cut to and from each shot where we **want** but only when we **can**.

Once two actors were filmed walking across a field. The camera tracked alongside them shooting two different setups: one was a two-shot looking one way (one character nearer the camera) and then the other way (positions reversed). One of the actors was smoking, and the director and editor were astounded to see that he took the same puff on the same syllable of the speech all through the long scene. This meant that they could **always** cut from one shot to the other, and they could cut to the best moments, not just cut when they could.

How much better it is to be this sort of actor. It is protection for you to go into a shoot with your bits of business already mapped out and rehearsed.

It can be a great distraction to you and your interpretation if you are acting in a meal scene, the camera pointed over your shoulder toward the other actor, and then the camera turns around; and just before you are about to launch into your close-up speech, the continuity girl hands you a whole **sheaf** of notes about **when** you should lift the glass, take a mouthful, lean forward, etc. I have seen performances suffer from too many continuity notes being handed over—but they **have** to be given.

Some actors decide that getting all those continuity notes is too boring, so their solution is to keep their hands in their pockets all the time, eat nothing at a meal time, and never to smoke. It does, of course, make their lives **easier** on the shoot, but does it make their performances **better**? It is far preferable to work out business in advance, bring it into the shoot, and allow excellent continuity to add to the performance (and add to the number of times the editor can cut to you). Expert film actors as different as Michael Caine and Sir John Gielgud admit to extensive preparation—rearranging the furniture in their hotel rooms or laying out a table—and going over and over the moves or business until they are completely at ease with it all. On the shoot they can devote their time and talent to the important things, like sharing their best moments with the camera, rather than struggling to remember which hand picked up which spoon when.

If an actor already knows and appreciates the importance of the continuity, then he can turn it to his advantage.

For example, an editor likes to cut from one picture to another with a large piece of business. It helps to motivate the cut and disguises some of the inevitable mismatches in continuity, for unless you are working on a project that can take infinite pains, it is almost impossible to cut from three people at one angle, to the same people from a different angle, and find a moment when all the heads, shoulders, arms, hands, etc. are perfectly matching for a good continuous cut.

So the editor looks for that piece of business, and the experienced actor finds that his character just happens to want to do a nice big movement or gesture just before a moment he thinks would be good to be featured in. And he has helped the editor decide by giving him some cut-motivating business.

Wise actor.

Film versus video

In the old days, it was believed that a multicamera shoot recorded something a little more "truthful" than a single camera, since the actors and all their reactions and bits of business would be in real time. Nowadays, this is not considered true at all.

With a single camera, cutting from one moment of action to the same moment on another shot does not always mean cutting at the "truthful" moment. It may be necessary to keep certain bits in twice to give the **impression** of reality. Everyone knows that you may be some feet away from another actor in one shot and touching shoulders with him in the closer shot that will be directly cut to.

Editing Secrets

- more reactions can give the editor more choices (to cut to you)

- give plenty of eye flashes to the editor

- good continuity gives more chances to the editor to cut to your best bits

- put in a nice bit of business before a moment you want on screen

- don't think about reality, think about creating the appearance of reality

Multicamera shoots in these days of modern editing equipment, where even the most hurried drama gets a chance in the editing room, are now adopting the same techniques. In the old days, editing a multicamera shoot was mostly just joining the scenes together and replacing the odd shot that didn't work. Now, edits are tightened, actors' pauses are taken out, all the tricks of a single camera edit session are applied in part to the multicamera edit.

I was editing a scene where two actors were in an embrace and then turned to come into the kitchen. The embrace was in a tight two-shot, and as they turned I cut to a long shot from the kitchen, to get their turn and then their walk toward the camera. In the edit, the editor removed a chunk of the "turn" from the second shot (adding up to one-third of a second) to allow the turn to look "natural." It was by now **not** "natural"—the actors were turning not in real time but in "screen" time. This is yet another example of how shooting reality does not always give the **impression** of reality.

Watching an editing session

If you ever get the chance to sit in on an editing session, **take the opportunity**. By watching what is kept (and what is not), what is effective (and what is not), you will quickly see what is required to be a good performer on the screen, and you be will able to put these ideas into practice the next time you are in front of the camera. A fractional difference, such as the slight change in Bette Davis's eyes at the beginning of this chapter, can make a huge difference to what the shot means to us the viewers. Don't, whatever you do, say anything in the edit session, however much you may be tempted. Bite your tongue, for any comments you may make will usually be about getting more of you onto the screen and will annoy the editor, as well as feed the belief that actors are only interested in their close-ups.

I know that there are those actors who insist that they "never watch their performances" or "never watch the rushes/dailies." That is like a stage actor paying no attention at all to any audience reaction or giving his best performance after the audience has gone home. (All right, I know there are **some** who do that). Be proud of your craft: learn all you can about it, and enjoy practicing it.

End Matters

EPILOGUE

A good workman has a good box of tools and knows how to use every one. An expert workman also knows **which** tool to use **when**. Everything in the toolbox is not used on every job at every moment.

In this book I have tried to teach you the whys and wherefores of different techniques for the screen. Not all of them will be of use to all of you all the time, but they should give you a better range of choices to make when faced with differing problems of acting in front of the camera.

A great deal of professional acting nowadays means working on the screen, yet those connected with training are mostly past and current stage performers. Even those who have screen experience often have only had it in front of the camera, but they do not always know what goes on behind the scenes that influences what goes onto the screen itself.

It is wonderful to have a strong belief about styles of acting. It goes wrong, however, when it becomes religious in its intensity, and the belief grows that there is only one true faith. Just as many find different ways to worship, so there are different ways to act.

When you started to drive a stick shift car, you wondered how on earth it was possible to talk and change gears at the same time. It all seemed very difficult, and yet soon you were chatting away, weaving in and out of traffic. Changing gears has become so automatic you barely notice or think about it.

That is how screen acting can be when you are experienced. It **will** feel a little odd at the start. Just as you did not give up driving because it felt strange at first, so feeling strange while screen acting should not put you off, but should lead to more study, practice—and wild enjoyment!

You may well find that for a long period of time you will not be bothered with these techniques, that your natural acting is fine and just what the screen likes and needs. Then one day you will be asked to do something technical "raise that book right up into frame," and if you are not ready for it, the demands of the screen can ruin your concentration and acting. It is for these moments that you need these secrets!

THE FAMOUS SCREEN ACTING CHECKLIST

© Patrick Tucker, 1994

Take these pages out—cut down the dotted line—so you can re-read them when waiting around on a set. Try not to show them to others—after all, you had to buy this book for its secrets—so should they!

A. Etiquette

1. Keep going until the director shouts "Cut!" Then keep on acting for a bit.

2. If you mess up a line, still keep going so it is the director who calls a halt to the proceedings, if he chooses to do so.

3. Do not stop a take for **any** reason (except injury or death).

4. Never look directly into the camera lens unless you are specifically asked to do so.

5. Never ask the director what size of shot it is. (Ask the camera operator.).

6. Being in the right place is often more important than saying the right line.

7. Keep your concentration and eyelines all through the tedium of lineup and rehearsal; it helps both your fellow actors **and** the crew.

8. An actor only has status between "Action!" and "Cut!" (But a star has it at all times between "Good morning darling!" and "That's a wrap for today—will we see you tomorrow?")

9. Never say "No"; say "Maybe." Never say you do not want to play a role; say (or have your agent say—that is what he is for) that you are unavailable.

B. The Lens

1. Let the lens be a magnet that draws your face toward it wherever it is.

2. Don't just cheat an eyeline, **motivate** it.

3. If both your eyes cannot "see" the camera lens, your face will appear to be obscured.

4. Keep on the imaginary "red carpet" that stretches out from the front of the camera. Remember, shots are composed in depth.

5. In a deep three-shot, put the lens (and not yourself) in the middle of the gap.

6. If you have trouble hitting a mark, line up two objects at the final position you have to hit.

7. Shoulders angled toward the camera often look better than straight-on ones.

C. The Frame

1. Cheat business and hands up into the "hot" area.

2. The size of shot predicts the style of acting within the frame:

> Long shot = "back of the balcony"—big gestures.
>
> Medium Shot = "intimate theater"—theatrical truth and reality.
>
> Medium Close-Up = "real reality"—the real thing.
>
> Extreme Close-Up = "pillow relationship"—just think it, and put all your energy **and** concentration into your face.

3. Be prepared to stand embarrassingly close when acting and speaking with other characters.

4. There is no reality outside the frame; time and/or distance outside it may be expanded or contracted.

D. Vocal

1. Only project as far as your microphone; check where it is before each take.

2. Intensity can be shown by increasing pace, **not** volume.

3. When the camera is moving with you, talk fast but move slowly.

4. If you are told to tone it all down, try reducing **only** your volume but keeping the scale of your gestures. (The "over the top" bit was probably your voice.)

5. Be aware that when using a strong accent that is not your own, you will tend to speak louder than usual—don't.

6. With a studio audience, if they can hear you without the benefit of micro-phones, you are speaking too loudly.

7. Never project louder than the star (or a regular in a series). They set the style for the program.

8. When speaking at low levels, do not lose your sparky energy or adopt a very slow pace.

9. At low levels of speaking, all other sounds seem too loud, so be careful with all footsteps, clattering cups, newspaper rustling—even breathing.

10. As the scene builds, you would expect the voices to rise. But since the shots are liable to get tighter, you have to square the circle by getting more intense—and quieter—at the same time.

11. Gently inquire if you are going to be in a contained two-shot, or if they are going to cross-cut with reverses, in which case be prepared to be asked **not** to overlap dialogue.

E. Acting

1. Your main acting note is that **you** were given the part, so work your looks, personality and background into your performance.

2. The shots the director chooses are in themselves acting notes, so obey their implicit instructions:

   Long shot = let your **body** do the talking.

   Reaction shot = **do** a reaction.

   Two-shot = **react** as you listen to the other actor.

   Close-up = put your thoughts onto your **face**.

   Close up of your hand holding a prop = put your acting and thoughts into **that**.

3. Do **all** your acting for an **Audience of One**—the camera.

4. Create good acting reasons for all your pieces of business (including camera-motivating ones).

5. The lines should fit you like a glove. If they don't, and you don't have the rehearsal time to create the character who would say those lines, then ask to change the dialogue.

6. Find positive ways of communicating negative thoughts.

7. Give yourself something to do **after** a shot ends. This will keep your face alive right to the end of the take.

8. Let your inner voice give you those continuous instructions that silent movie actors got from their directors' megaphones.

9. Let an acting impulse that would lead to a move on stage lead to a gesture or look on the screen.

10. When the camera is on you in a single shot, it is as if you were alone on a stage and all the other performers were in the wings: **now** how do you act?

F. Reactions and Business

1. React before you speak, and react to the upcoming thought. (This is best done on the intake of breath before a line.)

2. React **while** others are speaking—on screen we watch the listening person.

3. The best moments are nonverbal ones—so give yourself **time**.

4. Learn all your lines and business in advance of the shoot **very, very** well. During the shoot you will be concentrating on all the **new** things, such as remembering camera angles and hitting marks. (But also remember that you may be required to change lines and business at the very last moment, so be flexible, in a **very** cooperative way!)

5. Pace is continuous events, **not** continuous speaking.

6. Fully motivate any large reactions. Don't reduce your size, increase your believability.

7. Remember the camera cannot follow fast movements, so lift that cup slowly, gently rise up out of that chair.

8. In a multicamera studio a red light means the camera is on, so keep a reaction on your face until it has been sampled by that camera.

9. Eyes can be very effective. Try looking up as well as down, especially when "listening" to another character. (Some try looking from one eye to the other.)

10. At an interview and reading, plan at least one major reaction in the middle of a reading. Remember to react during the "feed" lines, and to keep your eyes **up**.

G. The Editor

1. The better your continuity, the easier it is for the editor to cut to you for your best moments.

2. Editors like to cut on movements, so put some in before one of your important bits of acting.

3. Mark changes of thought with such pieces of business.

4. During a speech, look at the other characters. The editor needs your "eyeflashes" to motivate cuts.

5. Reactions don't have to be logical or consistent. The editor is only looking for a slice of a good reaction, and several different ones give him a better choice (to cut to you!).

H. Final Thoughts

1. To come across as truthful and believable needs both talent **and** technique.

2. Don't panic over any problem. There has never been a trouble-free shoot, and anyway tomorrow's problem is already in the mail.

3. Don't do today's job as an audition for tomorrow's. Do it because **this** is what you wanted to do today. (Well it is, isn't it?) And when you are out of work you will regret not concentrating absolutely on today's acting.

4. All rules are made to be broken—so **know which rules you are breaking**! (And have a very good reason for doing so.)

5. Screen acting is going to be a very important part of your career, so find out how to **enjoy** and relish it all. If you allow it, it can (and **should**) be a lot of fun.

6. Do you have any items that have helped you but are not included here? Send them to me, and they will appear here next time. (And you'll get a free copy and acknowledgment!)

ACTING EXERCISES

The relevant exercises and practical examples I have developed over the years are scattered throughout this book, and for those of you who are interested in teaching these, or in practically developing your own talents, I thought it would be nice to put them all here together.

Be careful that you don't just do an exercise without understanding the reason behind it.

The equipment needed is not so elaborate. As a basic minimum you need a camcorder and a television monitor to show the results. Moving up-market, you could have one camera, one video recorder and one monitor. But you **do** need to have a separate microphone (and those of you who have read from the beginning will know exactly why).

Do **not** use the microphone attached to the camcorder, for this will give you the wrong sound for the picture. Get a separate microphone, or remove the camcorder mike and use that with an extension lead, and attach it (ideally) to a fishpole to become your boom (a long pole with a cushioned mount at the end to accept the microphone). A fishpole can be bought for a reasonable sum if you get an aluminum one and somewhat more if you get the useful collapsible carbon fiber one.

If you do not have access to a fishpole, then a microphone can be attached to something as simple as a broom handle; the problem is that the microphone will pick up any and all vibrations, and you should try to find a way of cushioning the microphone from the pole. Manufacture something out of foam rubber or elastic bands.

Get everyone in the group to experience the different jobs needed to record screen work, and learn to appreciate the work each department does. Discover the teamwork necessary for anything good to be put onto a screen.

Camera person Operates the camera, pointing it in the right direction, and getting the correct size of shot by adjusting the zoom lens. Often, it will not be appropriate to leave the camera on auto-focus (where it focuses on the nearest object), and as it is tricky for an inexperienced operator to point, zoom **and** focus, an **assistant camera person** can be used, whose job is to look at the monitor and keep the camera focused on what-ever should be in focus at that time (maybe the actor farthest away, with the nearer actors out of focus).

Boom operator Holds the boom, and thus the microphone, at the correct dis-tance from the actor so that good sound is obtained and the boom is not in shot. During the technical rehearsal, the microphone should be dipped in and out of shot so the boom operator can gauge where the edge of frame is. The operator should always boom the picture that she sees; for example, if there are two people talking, one closer to the camera than the other, it is the **nearer** person who should be boomed, since the viewer would expect the person standing farther off to sound more distant than the one standing much nearer. A very common fault is to record a scene and discover there was no sound. (I speak from bitter experience.) A good way around this is for the boom operator to wear headphones that tell her what sound is being picked up. (These can also indicate if there is a lot of "rustle" from the boom and micro-phone itself, drowning out the actors' voices.)

Floor manager Or first assistant, runs the floor, puts marks down where the director or actor wants, prompts during rehearsals where necessary, hands properties to the actors (sometimes lying on the floor and handing up a prepared cup of tea, sheaf of papers, etc.), calls out the shot and take numbers.

Technician Operates the video recorder, if a separate one is being used. Is responsible for seeing that the tape is actually moving and that sound is coming in from the microphone, as shown by the meter, if you have one.

Director Plans, organizes, starts and stops each take.

Actors If it is not a fully professional setup, it is possible that the actors can actually **see** the monitor as they present their per-formances to the screen. They must **not get into the habit of looking at the monitor** since professionally, they will **not** be able to see a picture of their scene while they are acting it.

It is a good idea if the group gets used to using a regular procedure and vocabulary for starting each shot, such as:

Director: "Roll tape." Technician/camcorder operator turns on machine.

Technician: (Or camcorder operator) "Running," when she sees numbers changing, sees the machine actually working.

Boom operator: (or technician, if there are no headphones) "Sound," when she can hear sound coming through from the set.

Floor manager: "Shot one, take one," (and next time, "Shot one, take two," etc.) This is the "slate" at the head of each shot, and in the movies it is that famous clapper board so beloved of Hollywood.

Director: "Action!" It is such fun to say this for the first time. Actually, I still enjoy saying it.

Actors: Act.

Director: "Cut!" Actors stop acting; everyone looks to the director to see if the whole thing is to be repeated, or whether we all move on to the next shot.

The other piece of equipment that I find invaluable for classwork is a frame. This should be the size of a television screen and should allow everyone to see what happens when a frame is put around a person, two people, three people, etc. I have made a collapsible one out of wood, but once when I was without it, I found I could make a very acceptable frame that illustrated all the points I needed by making four long rolls from newspapers, joining them together to make the correctly sized screen and then flattening the whole thing.

A word of warning: class members can often ruin a take by talking, even laughing out loud at what someone does (and so get their voices onto the sound track). It is easy to forget that when the camera is recording, this is not a rehearsal—this is the real thing, a performance.

The exercises are grouped under their Chapter headings.

Chapter One—Screen versus Stage

1. Get the class to write down what they would do differently, if anything, in acting for the screen as opposed to acting for the stage. Store the results for reading back when the rest of the exercises have been done.

2. Hold up a frame, and have someone watch it from about eight feet away. Make actors stand as far away it as is necessary for the observer to see them in the frame as long shot, medium shot, medium close-up, close-up and big close-up. If possible, sit in a theater with the frame, to see what seat corresponds to what size shot.

3. Try to convey different emotions at the different distances, to see what techniques are needed. Get couples to stand at different distances to act "I hate you!" or "I love you!" and to see what changing the distance does.

4. Play a scene "as if in real life"; play the same scene "as if on stage"; play the same scene with the frame, and see what happens to the screen version.

Chapter Two—Film versus Television

5. Shoot someone saying a simple line, and give different directions to each take. See the differences, and spot if the actor can remember which one he did when—**and** if the actor can spot the "best" one that the audience preferred.

6. Watch a movie blockbuster on a television screen. Get the class to note what moments are different from what they remembered from the big screen. Decide which scenes work better or worse for the size of screen.

7. Watch some television scenes, and have the class imagine they are being shown on a huge movie-house screen. Investigate if there are any scenes or shots that would be better or worse by being projected at this size.

Chapter Three—The Frame

8. Put a frame around ordinary activities: writing a letter, drinking a cup of tea, knitting a sweater, repairing a radio. Then "cheat" the activity until all the important bits are in the frame—and see what the actor has to do to achieve this.

9. Take famous stills from movies or television programs, and get the actors to reproduce each moment **exactly**. Use blocks, cushions or whatever to achieve the correct result, and compare the "look" of the result with the "feelings" of the actors composing the picture.

10. Do ordinary, everyday scenes such as, "Can you tell me the way to the Station?" but stage them so that both faces can be seen in the frame that is held up to them. Insist that they get right into the frame, regardless of embarrassment, and then make sure they do not act what they actually feel but what they are supposed to be feeling.

11. Pick moments from TV shows or movies (preferably by videotaping them) and get the class to reproduce the relationships and moments **exactly**.

12. Videotape each member of the group in close-up. Play back the results to see what is missing when only the head and shoulders can be seen, as opposed to seeing them full-length in real life.

Chapter Four—The Camera

13. Record thirty seconds of the actors doing anything previously learned. Play back the results: note the vocal levels, the degree of stiffness, the **effect** that being on camera has on them, and see if it tends to drown their best moments.

14. Play back the thirty seconds recorded from the previous exercise. Use a small masking device (I use an ordinary kitchen spatula) to block out the eyes and mouth, and see what the effect is when this area (about 10% of the screen) is missing from the playback. Did any of the actors use the rest of the screen to communicate with their audience?

15. Practice doing little moves of the eyes, head or hands to **motivate** the camera to move off to another person. Practice moving slowly across the room to **motivate** the camera to zoom in or out on a figure in the center of the screen.

16. Have actors walk past the camera as it pans with them, varying the rates of walking and of talking. Have them act very angry or very sad, and **see** what is needed from the actors to make the camera record the appropriate effect. Practice talking fast and walking slow.

17. Record a group of three or four actors, rearranging them until they look good on camera, then compare the look on the floor with the look on the screen. Experiment with different staging, so the actors start to feel what is "good" screen staging and what is not. Try acting "on the red carpet" to see how different it is from theater staging.

Chapter Five—Reactions and Business

18. Shoot everyone doing just thirty seconds for the camera. See how few gestures and reactions they put in. Repeat with many reactions and ges-

tures. See how **few** words an actor can say, while still being entertaining and interesting.

19. Record each actor doing a series of unemotional bits of business: swallowing, clenching the back teeth so the muscles bulge in the cheek, brushing the hair off the forehead, sneering. Play back the results, but this time add dialogue that makes the gestures seem a response to the lines just given.

20. Shoot everyone saying a short speech, but insist that they all react **before** speaking. Compare how this comes across without such reactions.

21. Shoot each person just listening to another talking. Shoot again, asking the listener to do too much, and find out how much **is** "too much."

22. Shoot a scene where the object is to see how many different things the actor can do with a pencil, a telephone, a chair. See how different bits of business suit different actors.

23. Shoot the silent movie exercise. Choose an actor to be shot playing a hugely melodramatic moment. Repeat the exercise, but this time shout out instructions (using a megaphone?) for her to obey, keeping the instructions one on top of another in a continuous stream. Play back and compare the results.

24. Record some examples of television commercials that have many changing expressions of the performers. Get the class to reproduce them—exactly. Both in scale and in frequency, get them to feel what it is like to act the way that professional actors do on the screen.

Chapter Six—Sound and Vocal Levels

25. Play scenes with a high emotional content, using very little voice but a lot of everything else. If necessary, the director should put his face within six inches of the actor, and then get him to "perform" in a passionate way. Find out what it is like to have to work this way.

26. Watch some famous film or television scenes, and then reenact them using all the emotions **and vocal levels** that were in the original. Be precise about the vocal levels, for they will often seem to be other than they were.

27. Have an actor play a scene that starts calm and ends up with a raging emotion. Shoot it starting in long shot, then zoom in during the speech to end with a close-up. See what adjustments are necessary to make the whole speech effective.

28. Set up the actors in couples to have private conversations seated some three feet apart. Repeat the exercise keeping the seats three feet apart, but now the actors must project to the other person **as if** he were only six inches away. They must **not** slow down the rate of their delivery. (They will probably also laugh, it seems so peculiar.)

Chapter Seven—Typecasting

29. Get each actor in turn to read out the one-line description they think would be written about them after a short interview. Have a vigorous discussion and truth-telling session. (If these one-liners are videotaped, it often happens that because the actors are concentrating on something new, most of what has been taught already goes out the window. The moral—something new tends to drive them back to what they know: stage acting).

30. Get everyone to come before the camera, and record them saying "I'd vote for her." Play back the results, and everyone shout out who the "she" is that each character would be voting for. See how the look (coupled with the way they are dressed) affects how they come across, and note that there is not necessarily a connection with how the actors themselves would actually vote.

31. Shoot everyone in profile, and tell them that when there is a click of the fingers, they must turn toward the camera with no thoughts whatsoever in their heads. Play back the results to see just how much information is in the change from profile to full face.

32. A nice variation of the previous exercise is to add some made-up dialogue just before they turn their heads, to see again how much is conveyed just by the changing looks.

33. Film everyone in close-up as they goggle their eyes, lick their lips, clench their teeth, flare their nostrils, blink and flutter their eyes, swallow, etc. Play back the results, and work out which facial gesture suits which actors best.

34. Put a theatrical photograph of someone in front of the camera, so everyone can see the result on the screen. Get the actor whose picture it is to perform anything **in the manner of the photograph**. The audience critiques until a performance is obtained that matches the look. Sometimes this can be helped by adjusting how much of the photo is to be seen. The conclusion is often that the actor does not like the performance that matches the photo. In that case, she should get another photo.

Chapter Eight—Acting

35. Recreate original theater conditions, and present a medieval mystery on a tabletop, a Shakespeare snippet in daylight, a Restoration piece to a candlelit room, and a melodramatic moment lit by one candle with the audience at least thirty feet away. Sample and see what styles of acting are needed for the different audience/actor relationships and for what can or cannot be seen. Extend this practice to silent screen acting: what is the relationship and what can be seen, and then extend it into spoken screen acting.

36. Get everyone to practice a sneeze done with the lips, a laugh done with vibrating the diaphragm, a cry done the same way, tears produced by some eye-watering vapor (onions?). Record the results and practice until the moves come across as convincing.

Chapter Nine—Auditions

37. Have each actor practice coming in, shaking hands and saying, "Hello!" Grade each one. Get the class to grade each other. Get practiced at this basic of any audition.

38. Record each person coming to a mark and announcing her name and agent (this can be a fictitious name) into the lens. Again, grade each person about how well she announces her name. (Actors hate being graded, but it will happen to them in auditions, so it is useful to get used to the concept that yes, people are going to sit and give them marks as to their effectiveness.)

39. Record some little two- or three-handed improvisations, seeing how at first most will go into "theatric" staging. Re-do the exercise until they can all do "filmic" staging as they improvise.

40. Repeat the previous exercise, but this time record no sound. Play back the results, and repeat so that all the information that was in the improvised dialogue is now in their bodies and gestures.

41. Ask each actor to come to a mark, say her name and agent into the camera, then bite into an imaginary piece of chocolate and say "Wow!" Play back the results, and cruelly decide who was "best." Repeat as often as necessary.

42. Find current commercials on television that demand similar deeply committed performances, and play the originals to the class. Then get **them** to do it.

43. Record each actor doing five distinct reactions in five seconds. If necessary, call out the changes to the actor, silent movie style.

44. Practice a cold reading with a camera on the face, and see how much can be done in the "listening" phase of the audition. If the same reading is given to each actor, have her do the interview and reading without anyone else present, then play back the results so all can see (and judge) the relative effectiveness of each actor.

Chapter Ten—Rehearsals and Technicals

45. Have a read-through of a scene with everyone sitting around a table **giving a close-up vocal level performance**. Experience and practice how to do this, and notice the differences in the expressions on the faces when they are speaking at low levels.

46. Rehearse small scenes, with many marks to hit and moves to make. Get used to the extreme technicality that can be demanded from such a shoot.

47. If the equipment is available, do some longer scenes with two cameras cutting between them during the scene, so the actors get used to longer takes and to the multicamera experience.

Chapter Eleven—Directing Actors for the Screen

48. Play a little scene with two actor facing each other. Get them to repeat the scene, but this time with one speaking over the other's shoulder. Repeat with different ways of not looking at each other.

49. Shoot an over the shoulder two-shot of a short, intimate scene. Shoot it again as a close-up but with only one actor there, playing to an invisible partner. (It can be a piece of paper with eyes drawn on it.) Play back and compare the results.

Chapter Twelve—Announcers and the Art of Being Interviewed

50. Have the actors each bring in an official photograph and a "favorite" snapshot. Put each official photograph in front of a camera lens, and get the performer to do a speech in the manner of the photograph. Get the "favorite" snapshot from the participant, and (using the macro lens on the camcorder if necessary) blow it up to be seen on screen. Now have the announcer give a speech, but this time in the manner of the snapshot. It will usually be better, more relaxed, more **them.**

51. Dangerous exercise: get the participants (helped by the audience if necessary) to identify those aspects of themselves they are least happy with, least proud of. Then get them to do a speech or interview presenting these negative aspects positively.

52. Get the participants to take part in an interview situation, concentrating not just on their replies, but on "active listening."

53. Get each member of the class to do a long speech, and see how long he can go on without putting in a full stop. Pauses are possible, but the voice must never come to a downward inflection.

Chapter Thirteen—The Shoot

54. Shoot a little scene with many technical problems. Play back the results—and immediately shoot the scene again. This allows the actor to put in practice what she has just learned. (All too often in the professional realm, it is so long after a shoot that an actor gets to see what she has done, that when viewing the result, she has forgotten what it was that led her to do it like that in the first place.)

55. Shoot little moments of actors coming into two- and three-shots, with them having to find their mark and making it look as if that is what the character wanted to do. Shoot the actors **motivating** a look downward to check a mark, an edge sideways to get into shot, holding a cup up high into shot and keeping it there.

Chapter Fourteen—The Editor and Editing

56. Shoot a two-handed scene with munching of sandwiches. Shoot it again from the other side, and check how good the continuity was. Practice until members of the class can do complicated business and **repeat it exactly**.

57. Shoot one actor doing lots of differing reactions to a speech by another. Play it back, and only show, say, the middle reaction out of a sequence. See how reactions can stand on their own when only used as a quick cutaway.

Epilogue

58. Read back what the class **thought** screen acting was.

BIBLIOGRAPHY

Books Relating to Screen Acting

Here is a list of the books I have consulted—books which are on my shelves —about screen acting. The ones I have found particularly useful and think you might like a lot I have marked with an *, but this is purely a personal opinion. You may well find great insights in any of the following books (some of whose opinions I personally could not agree less with).

Books on Acting: on Film/Television Acting

Acting for Film and TV, by Leslie Abbott. (Belmont, Calif.: Star Publishing, 1994).

Acting for the Camera, by Tony Barr. (Boston: Allyn & Bacon Inc., 1982).

Acting Hollywood Style, by Foster Hirsch. (New York: Harry N. Abrams, Kobal Collection, 1991).

Acting in Film, by Michael Caine. (New York: Applause Theatre Book Publishing, 1990).

Acting in Television Commercials for Fun and Profit, by Squire Fridell. (New York: Crown, 1987).

Acting in the Cinema, by James Naremore. (Berkeley and Los Angeles, Calif.: University of California Press, 1988).

Acting One, by Robert Cohen. (Palo Alto, Calif.: Mayfield, 1978).

The Actor's Survival Guide for Today's Film Industry, by Renee Harman. (Englewood Cliffs, N.J.: Prentice-Hall Inc., 1984).

American Film Acting, by Richard A. Blum. (Ann Arbor, Mich.: UMI Research Press, 1984).

Film Acting, by Mary Ellen O'Brien. (New York: Arco Publishing, 1983).

Film and Television Acting, by Ian Bernard. (Stoneham, Mass.: Butterworth-Heinemann, 1993).

Film Technique and Film Acting, by V. I. Pudovkin. (New York: Bonanza Books, 1949).

A Guide For Actors New to Television, by Tristan de Vere Cole. (Longmead, Dorset: Element Books Ltd., 1985).

On Screen Acting, by Edward and Jean Porter Dmytryk, (Boston :Focal Press, 1984).

Sanford Meisner On Acting, by Sanford Meisner and Dennis Longwell. (New York: Vintage Books, 1987).

Screen Acting, by Brian Adams. (Beverly Hills: Lone Eagle, 1987).

"Some Notes on Film Acting," by Lawrence Shaffer. *Sight and Sound* 42, no. 2, (London: B.F.I., 1973).

TV Acting: A Manual for Camera Performances, by Larry Kirkman et al. (New York: Hastings, 1979).

Books by or about Actors: Acting Training

Actors on Acting, edited by Toby Cole and Helen Krish Chinoy, (New York: Crown, 1970).

Actors talk about Acting, edited by Lewis Funke and John E. Booth. (New York: Avon Books, 1961).

Actors Talk: About Styles of Acting, by John D. Mitchell. (Midland, Mich.: Northwood Institute Press, 1988).

Being an Actor, by Simon Callow. (New York: Grove Press, 1988).

The Complete "About Acting," by Peter Barkworth. (London: Heinemann, 1980).

Confessions of an Actor, by Laurence Olivier. (New York: Simon & Schuster, 1992).

The Job of Acting, by Clive Swift. (London: Harrap, 1976).

Masters of the Stage, edited by Eva Mekler. (New York: Grove Weidenfeld, 1989).

The New Breed—Actors Coming of Age, by Karen Hardy and Kevin J. Koffler. (New York: Holt, 1988).

The New Generation of Acting Teachers, edited by Eva Mekler. (New York: Penguin Books, 1987).

On Acting, by Laurence Olivier. (New York: Simon & Schuster, 1986).

Papers on Acting, edited by Brander Matthews. (New York: Hill and Wang, 1958).

People Will Talk, by John Kobal. (New York: Aurum Press, 1991).

The Player—A Profile of an Art, by Lillian Ross & Helen Ross. (New York: Limelight Editions, 1984).

Snakes and Ladders, by Dirk Bogarde. (New York: Penguin, 1988).

Star Acting: Gish, Garbo, Davis, by Charles Affron. (New York: Dutton, 1977).

Stars, by Richard Dyer. (London: B.F.I., 1982).

Working Actors, by Richard A. Blum and Laurence Frank. (Boston: Focal Press, 1989).

Books about the Film/Television Medium (with references to acting)

An American Odyssey, Elia Kazan edited with Michel Ciment. (London: Bloomsbury Publishing, 1988).

Billy Wilder in Hollywood, by Maurice Zolotov. (New York: Limelight Editions, 1987).

Directing for Film and Television, by Christopher Lucas. (New York: Doubleday, 1985).

Directing the Film, by Eric Sherman. (Los Angeles: Acrobat Books, 1988).

Film Art, by David Bordwell and Kristin Thompson. (New York: McGraw-Hill, 1990).

Film Lighting, by Kris Malkiewicz and Barbara J. Gryboski. (New York: Prentice Hall, 1986).

The Film-Makers Art, by Haig P. Manoogian. (New York: Basic Books, 1966).

The Filmmaker's Handbook, by Edward Pincus and Steven Ascher. (New York: New American Library, 1984).

Filmmaking: The Collaborative Art, by Donald Chase. (Boston: Little, Brown, 1975),

From Reverence to Rape, by Molly Haskell. (Chicago: University of Chicago Press, 1987).

Getting the Part, by Judith Searle. (New York: Simon & Schuster, 1991).

Inner Views: Filmmakers in Conversations, by David Breskin. (Boston: Faber and Faber, 1992).

Interviews with Film Directors, by Andrew Sarris. (New York: Avon Books, 1967).

Masters of Light, by Dennis Schaefer. (Berkeley and Los Angeles: University of California Press, 1985).

Off Camera, by Richard Levinson and William Link. (New York: New American Library, 1986).

On Directing Film, by David Mamet. (New York: Penguin Books, 1992).

Selected Works, by Sergei Eisenstein. (London: B.F.I., 1991).

Take One, by Jack Kuney. (New York: Praeger, 1990).

The Technique of Television Production, by Gerald Millerson. (London: Focal Press, 1990).

The Television Program, by Edward Stasheff, Rudy Bretz, John Gartley and Lynn Gartley. (New York: Hill and Wang, 1976).

TV Director/Interpreter, by Lewis Colby. (New York: Hastings, 1990).

Other Useful References

Another Way of Telling, by John Berger and Jean Mohr. (New York: Pantheon Books, 1982).

Atlas of Facial Expression, by Stephen Rogers Peck. (New York: Oxford University Press, 1987).

Comics and Sequential Art, by Will Eisner. (Guerneville, Cal.: Eclipse Books, 1990).

Dictionary of Film and Television Terms, edited by Virginia Oakey. (New York: Barnes & Noble, 1983).

Fellini's Faces, edited by Christian Strich. (New York: Holt, Rinehart & Winston, 1982).

Frame Analysis, by Erving Goffman. (Boston: Northeastern University Press, 1986).

Mannerisms of Speech and Gestures in Everyday Life, by Sandor S. Feldman. (New York: International Universities Press, 1969).

To the Heart of the Storm, by Will Eisner. (Princeton, Wis.: Kitchen Sink Press, 1991).

What Do You Say After You Say Hello, by Eric Berne. (New York: Bantam, 1984).

BIOGRAPHIES

Patrick Tucker

The fourth child of a Professor of African languages, Patrick graduated as a physicist from the University of London, although he had by then become infected with the theater bug by acting in, and running a company on, the Edinburgh Festival Fringe. Appalled by the prospect of teaching Physics, he applied for a postgraduate course at Boston University as a joke, and to his surprise he won a scholarship to study directing there. He graduated two years later, having by then caught the directing bug and having directed at Texas' first Shakespeare Festival. He returned to England to find his directing talents unasked for, and so found work as: a stage electrician, a stage manager for a striptease club, a fellow Assistant Stage Manager with Cameron Mackintosh on the tour of *Oliver!*, a production manager in the West End, and finally—as a theater director in Rep.

Since his first professional production in 1968, he has directed over 130 plays in all forms of theater, from weekly repertory to the Royal Shakespeare Company. He was accepted by the BBC Television Directing program in 1976 and has subsequently directed more than 100 television programs, ranging from plays for the BBC to Shakespeare in Danish for Danish television, to many episodes of Liverpool's own soap opera *Brookside*.

Beginning with the RSC's American tour, Patrick started teaching Shakespeare and verse speaking. In going back to the basics (as any physicist should), he has developed his own unique approach based upon the cue scripts that Shakespeare's original actors would have used. He has taught his classes in the U.K., all over America and in the Far East.

He has developed his unique approach to television and film acting as a separate discipline and has presented these courses at the Drama Studio London with the graduate actors there since 1976 and in their California branch since the early 1980's. He has also lectured and taught all over the world, as well as directed plays in the United States, Canada, Denmark, Germany, Ireland, Israel, South Africa and South Korea, and has just been appointed Visiting Lecturer and Consultant to Liverpool John Moores University.

He lives with his actress partner Christine Ozanne in Chiswick, London, and has gained many insights and ideas from the screen work she has done over the years, including many commercials.

He says that if these ideas about screen acting seem unusual, wait until you hear about his approach to acting Shakespeare!

John Stamp

John Stamp is a freelance graphic designer living in Sunbury-on-Thames, England. He is married to a makeup designer and has a fifteen-year-old son and two married daughters. He was a student at the Hammersmith School of Building and Arts & Crafts. After National Service he had various jobs as a signwriter, pictorial artist and lettering artist.

He worked in the art department of Rank Screen Services and Paramount Pictures before joining ABC Television's graphic department in 1959. He worked for ABC Television/Thames Television from 1959 to 1990, seven years of which he served as head of the department.

He was artist in residence at Harrod's Poster and Print Department in 1986, exhibiting limited edition screen prints of the River Thames. Two of the prints were donated to the Leonard Cheshire Foundation and now hang in Park House, Sandringham, the country home of the Queen. In 1989 his "Famous Comedian Prints" were exhibited at the Dominion Cinema during the "Thames Silents" season, and in 1991 Thames Television held a retrospective exhibition of his work at the British Academy of Film and Television Arts, in honor of his work for ABC/Thames Television.

He is currently working on portraits of the twenty-nine founder members of the Theatre of Comedy for the Shaftesbury Theatre, London.

GLOSSARY

Here are a lot of the words and phrases that you may hear on a shoot, or see on the credits, and have always wondered what they mean, or what they refer to.

A/B: As before; particularly when a camera shot is to be the same as the previous one.

ACTION: What the director or first assistant says to start it all off.

ACTION PROPS: objects used or handled by actors, as opposed to ordinary props used for dressing (making it look good).

AFM: Assistant Floor Manager.

ANGLE: (see **CAMERA ANGLE**).

APERTURE: (see **F-STOP**).

ASPECT RATIO: the width to height ratio of a screen: 4 to 3 or 1.33:1 (Academy Aperture; all television until we get wide screen high definition TV); 1.66:1 (standard European wide screen); 1.85:1 (standard American wide screen); 2.35:1 (wide screen such as Panavision).

ASSISTANT DIRECTOR: the film director's main link, help (and bully boy).

ATMOSPHERE (also known as **ATMOS**): background sound recorded to smooth over possible unevenness in previously recorded background sounds from different shots.

AUTOCUE: (see **TELEPROMPTER**).

BACK LIGHT: lights the back of the actor as seen by the camera (to make him stand out from the background).

BACKGROUND ACTION: what all the extras (or supporting) artists do at the back of the shot in order to add the bustle of a crowd (and to get themselves noticed?)

BACKING TRACK: pre-recorded music to play when actors or musicians have to mime as they pretend to be actually playing.

BANANA: walking on a curved line, usually to allow the camera to see you earlier, or to prevent masking a fellow actor.

BARN DOOR: metal flaps attached to a light to stop its light spreading everywhere.

BCU: (see **ECU**).

BEAT: a small pause; also the unit of action much loved by Methodologists.

BEST BOY: chief assistant to the **GAFFER** (the chief electrician). Now, there are two titles you always wondered about in film credits.

BG: background.

BLOCKING THE SCENE: giving the moves for a scene (can apply both to actors and cameras); this is usually the first rehearsal.

BOOM: telescopic arm that holds the microphone above the action. It can also refer to a movable arm that attaches the camera to a **DOLLY.**

BOOM UP/DOWN: moving the microphone and its pole up and down; or the camera up/down.

BREAK: stop work for a while.

BUG EYE LENS: (see **FISH EYE LENS**).

BUSINESS: actions for an actor, usually involving a prop (sometimes, just **BIZ**).

CAMERA ANGLE: how high, low, and in which direction the camera is to point.

CAMERA CARDS: cards attached to a camera in a multicamera studio telling the operator what sort of shot (**MCU**) they should do at what time (shot number 114).

CAMERA TRAP: a hole in the scenery that can open up, so a camera can pop through to get the shot required and then disappear, with the scenery closing up so that no other camera will see where it was. This explains some of those "how on earth did they get that shot?" moments.

CANS: headphones.

CHEATING: the art and craft of doing something that is untrue, but appears true to the camera; as in "**CHEAT** your eyes towards camera; **CHEAT** your height by standing on this box".

CLAPPER BOARD: (see **CLAPSTICK BOARD**).

CLAPSTICK BOARD (also **CLAPPER BOARD**; **SLATE**): used for shot, scene and take number; it has a hinged bit that gives the satisfying clap at the start of a film sequence that helps them synchronize sound and picture in the editing. (What a pity that for video there is no such excitement.)

COLOR TEMPERATURE: the color a particular temperature is, especially in relation to lights used in filming; blue is much hotter than red.

CONTINUITY GIRL (also **SCRIPT GIRL**): the person who takes copious continuity notes (and Polaroids) so that the same business is done at the same time on all shots covering the same sequence.

CONTRAST RATIO: The difference between the brightest and darkest part of the picture. The human eye can cope with a **CONTRAST RATIO** of 100:1; film less than that, and video has the worst ratio of all—leading to difficulties in shooting video against a sunny window (the faces appear black).

COVERAGE: the number of shots taken to cover a whole scene; "Have you got enough **COVERAGE** for this sequence?"

CRAB: moving the camera sideways.

CRANE: a device that can raise the camera up; small ones take it to 6 feet up; giant ones take it up to look down on roofs. (These are very, very expensive, and producers are very reluctant to pay for them.)

CRANE UP/DOWN: moving the camera up and down.

CRAWL: very slow movement of the camera.

CROSS-CUTTING: to cut back and forth, especially between two unrelated scenes where things are happening simultaneously (as in cutting between the maiden tied to the railway tracks and the hero riding to rescue her).

CROSSING THE LINE: the crime of getting the geography wrong, and confusing the audience as to where everyone is. If two shots are taken of two actors talking to each other, then both cameras should be on the same side of an invisible line drawn between the two; if they are on opposite sides of the line, the two actors on screen will appear to be looking the same way, and so will not seem to be talking to each other at all.

CU: Close up.

CUE (also **Q**): the signal to start; often given by a frantic wave from one of the production team.

CUT: the point where one shot is changed for another, either by editing ("I want to **CUT** as you get up out of the chair") or in the multicamera studio ("I will **CUT** from the close-up on Camera 1 to the wide shot on Camera 3 as the door opens"); also used to stop everything, the opposite of **ACTION** (and said very angrily when things have gone wrong!)

CUTAWAY: usually a large shot of an object or bit of a person, used to give a close-up view of an important prop or face; also used to join two bits together that do not match too well; often used in documentaries.

CUTTER: (see **EDITOR**).

CYCLORAMA: curved backcloth, sometimes painted to pretend that a scene set inside a stuffy studio is on the wide open spaces of a beach.

DAILIES (also **RUSHES**): yesterdays's shots, rushed back to the shoot and shown to all interested people in case anything needs to be re-shot. (Actors usually don't get to see them.)

DAY-FOR-NIGHT: filming in daylight, and then adjusting the film so everyone thinks it is in fact at night. (Filmed with clear skies, underexposed, with a deep blue filter put on it.) Often ruined by having daytime birds happily flying across the "night" sky.

DEEP FOCUS: the system of wide lenses and small apertures that allow objects close and far away from the camera to be in focus. (Used to tremendous effect in Orson Welles' *Citizen Kane*.)

DEEPER: farther away.

DEPTH-OF-FIELD: the area that is in focus. On a bright day it can be very large, covering people at different distances from the camera; on a dull or dimly lit scene it can mean the actors having to hit their marks within ½ inch or they will be out of focus.

DISSOLVE: cross fading from one picture to another; it now has the symbolism of telling the audience that time has passed.

DFA: An alternative plan (as in "we need a different f—— arrangement!").

DOLLY: the truck on wheels that allows the camera to go charging about a studio, or off down some tracks.

DOLLYING: (also **TRACKING**; **TRUCKING**): the act of the camera doing such moving. "**DOLLY** in to the actors" will mean the camera will now come satisfyingly close to you. Directors love these moves almost as much as they love a mirror shot. (This fixation probably started at an early age with the young director's first train set.)

DOLPHIN ARM: (see **JIB ARM**).

DOUBLE: (see **TWO-SHOT**).

DOWNSTAGE: stolen from the stage world, meaning closer to the camera.

DROP-OUT: when the video tape loses contact with the recording apparatus, and there is a "flash" on the pictures; you always have to go again.

DRY: forgetting lines.

DRY RUN: running through a scene without all the effects that will be there on a **TAKE.**

DUBBING: transferring all the sound effects, music, replaced voices, etc. onto the finished product; also describes the process where your lovely voice is substituted by a completely different one when your performance is shown in Germany or Japan.

ECU (also **BCU**): Extreme close-up.

EDITOR: the person who joins the chosen bits of different takes together to make the finished program. In film she is also known as the **CUTTER.**

ELS: Extreme long shot.

END BOARD: Used when the **CLAPSTICK BOARD** is put on at the end of a take (maybe because it was forgotten, or because it was difficult to focus on it at the start). An **END BOARD** held upside down with the jaws open means the shot was done without any sound (**MOS**).

ESTABLISHING SHOT: the shot at the beginning of a scene that lets the audience know where they are. It can be a shot of the exterior of the house where everyone is talking inside; more interestingly it can be the first shot inside the house where the first speaker by an amazing coincidence just has to move all round the room, and so show the audience who else is there and what the room looks like.

EYELINE: the direction an actor takes when looking at the other actor. Directors (and actors) also like the camera to "get onto the **EYELINE**"—it means that both the eyes of the actor will be seen, and so they can do more with them.

F-STOP (also **APERTURE**): the size of the opening of the iris that lets light into the lens on the camera. The higher the number, the less light gets in.

FG: foreground.

FILL LIGHT: the light that fills in the shadows caused by the **KEY LIGHT**.

FINE CUT: the final assembly of the material. This is usually how it will be when shown to an audience.

FIRST ASSISTANT (see **ASSISTANT DIRECTOR**).

FISH EYE LENS: very wide angle lens. If you get too close to it, it makes you look as if you have a huge nose and small piggy eyes.

FISHPOLE: hand held portable boom.

FLAG: anything used to stop stray light getting to the camera and so creating a flare; also to take sunshine off actors.

FLOOR MANAGER: the director's link on a video studio floor, the equivalent to **FIRST ASSISTANT** or **ASSISTANT DIRECTOR** in the film world.

FLOOR PLAN: a bird's eye view of the scenery, with the positions of the cameras (and often the actors as well) marked in. This allows sound and lights to plan where to put their equipment to get the desired effects.

FLUFF: an actor tripping over a word, or saying the wrong one. (Sometimes called a **FLUB**.)

FOLEY: the replacement and addition of footsteps, animal noises, etc. to make a shot scene sound correct. Because there is often a lot of noise around (the sound of the camera itself moving) there is the need for a lot of this. Now you know what that mysterious **FOLEY** credit means that you have seen at the end of all movies; it is named after the individual who invented the process.

FREEZE FRAME: where the action is "frozen" by keeping one picture going; a good way of ending a scene if you can't think of a better one.

GAFFER: chief electrician.

GAFFER TAPE: heavy duty adhesive tape, used on a set for just about every fixing job.

GOLDEN HOUR: This is the twenty minutes or so of useful shooting time after the sun sets, when there is no direct sunshine but a wonderful glow to everything. Directors love to use this light, since it means everyone has to hang around all day, and the director only has to work for those twenty minutes (all right, I am sure there are other things going on).

GREENSMEN: those on the set or location who take care of all the greenery.

GRIP: transports and sets up the camera equipment, especially tracks.

HAIR IN THE GATE: usually heard after your best work. It means that there is a minute bit of fluff or emulsion in the camera, causing one of those black worms you occasionally see in the bottom of a piece of film—and it means you have to do the whole thing all over again. All film shots end therefore with "check the gate."

HAND-HELD: when the camera is hoisted onto the cameraperson's shoulder, and goes chasing all over following exciting action. It is often used to make things seem more "realistic" (that is, more wobbly, and like the sort of coverage coming from news cameras).

IDIOT CARDS: large sheets onto which the performer's lines are written (so that all that moody glancing away from their fellow actors is just in fact looking for their next line). Also used for a talk show host to tell them where the next "joke" is lurking.

IN THE CAN: a satisfactory recording or **TAKE**, as in "we have got it **IN THE CAN!"**

JIB ARM (also **DOLPHIN ARM**): an arm attached to the **DOLLY** that allows the camera to go up and down a reasonable amount.

JUICERS: (see **SPARKS**).

JUMP CUT: cutting from one picture to another with a huge difference in size, or in location, or in time continuity. The shock effect is the intention. It is also used as a term to describe two shots that the director wants to cut between, but the editor says no because there is a jump.

KEY LIGHT: the main light for an actor coming in over the top of the camera.

KILL (see also **STRIKE**): stop, or turn off; "**KILL** that light; **KILL** that lawn mower".

LEVEL: sound, as in "can you give us some more **LEVEL**?"

LINE UP: getting everything in position for a shot. Also what the cameras in a studio have to do together to get them balanced with each other.

LIP SYNC: the sound and movement of a speaker being correctly together. Occasionally when using the sound from one take with the picture of another, we briefly go out of **LIP SYNC** and you wonder how that happened.

LOCKED-OFF CAMERA: a camera that is fixed in position and shot size for a static shot. Sometimes used to denote a camera that is only shooting one particular thing or person (a child or baby) and will follow it wherever it goes.

LOOPING: running piece of film continuously through, so that the actor can get perfect **LIP SYNC** in **DUBBING** on new sounds by making many, many attempts.

LOSE THE LIGHT: when the natural daylight is about to become too dim, and everyone goes round shouting "we must get this shot **IN THE CAN** before we **LOSE THE LIGHT**."

LOW LOADER: a trailer onto which a car is put, and then pulled behind the truck with the camera, so that looking at the car and its occupants it looks as if they are driving through the countryside. It also explains why actors driving and acting are able to take their eyes off the road for so long—someone else is steering.

LS: long shot.

MARKS: tape or chalk to indicate where an actor should stand, or where they should come to after a move: "**MARK** those positions."

MASTER SHOT: a wide angle shot of the whole scene, done first so that everyone knows what lighting and positional moments have to be matched for all subsequent shots.

MCU: medium close-up.

MISE-EN-SCENE: a style of directing where the actors and camera are choreographed in a long sequence all in one shot. Also known as a developing shot, and very well liked by all show-off directors. (I particularly like doing them.)

MIXER: the person who mixes together the various inputs from the different microphones to get proper sound.

MONTAGE: a series of shots or short scenes to convey a whole period of time; as in shots of a train chugging across a map, interspersed with shots of ever larger auditoriums exploding with enthusiasm telling the story of the rise of a star.

MOS (also **MUTE**): made without sound. Romantics like to believe that it was early German directors in Hollywood saying "mitout sound", but it was more likely they were saying "mit-out sprache": we all prefer the first version.

MS: medium shot.

MULTICAMERA: a studio with anything from 3 to 7 video cameras all available to record the program, with the **SWITCHER** cutting from one camera to another.

MUTE: (see **MOS**).

NODDY: the shot of an interviewer nodding, cut in with the interview to make it look as if they agree with all that is being said. It is, of course, shot after the interviewee has long gone.

NTSC: (National Television System Committee) the color system for television used in the U.S. that was the first in the world. It is now also the least effective system (the penalty of being first). Rudely known in the trade as

Never The Same Color twice. (Other alternative systems are **PAL** and **SECAM.**)

OB: outside broadcast.

OFF-CAMERA [**OC**]: (see **OFF-SCREEN**).

OFF-LINE EDIT: video editing where the originals have been transferred (usually to VHS), and the rough edit is done on this material.

OFF-MIKE: lines given that have not been picked up clearly by the microphone. Often caused by the actor delivering the lines in a direction they did not do in rehearsal, or by the boom operator not getting the microphone into the correct position.

OFF-SCREEN [**OS**] (also **OFF-CAMERA**; and **OUT-OF-VISION**): an action or voice that is not seen on the screen but is referred to by the person on the screen; as in "can you **OOV** your lines from the bedroom?"

ON-LINE EDIT: video editing using the actual tape that was recorded during the shoot.

OOV: (see **OUT-OF-VISION**).

OTS: over the shoulder.

OTT: Over The Top; usually applied to an actor's performance (and usually only referring to the vocal level!)

OUT-OF-SYNC: the opposite of **LIP SYNC**, where the movement of the lips does not match the sounds heard.

OUT-OF-VISION [**OOV**]: (see **OFF-SCREEN**).

OUT-TAKE: those bits of a show that were originally mistakes (but now seem to be done on purpose to feed those programs that feature them as we watch actors and anchor persons fall over, forget lines, walk into walls, etc.).

OVERLAP: when your dialogue is said at the same time as another character. It is one of the most common reasons for "going again."

PAL: (Phased Alternating Line) the color system developed and used by Germany, and by most of Europe except France (naturally—see **SECAM**).

PAN: rotating the camera through an arc: "**PAN** left; **PAN** right; **PAN** up." Technically, it should be "**TILT UP**," but that is the way it goes.

PER DIEM: the expenses you get each day for food, sometimes accommodation; from the Latin (you knew that, didn't you?).

PILOT: the trial program of what we all hope will turn into a long running series. Many trek to Hollywood for the "**PILOT** season"; good luck! (You'll need it.)

POINT-OF-VIEW [POV]: what a character sees. Often the camera is put to get your **POV**, such as the dead body on the floor, the letter you are reading.

POLECAT: telescopic pole that can get jammed between floors and ceilings, between cross beams and walls, allowing lights to be hung where no light ought to go.

POSTPRODUCTION: all that happens to a production after the shooting has finished, such as editing, dubbing, special effects.

POV: (see **POINT-OF-VIEW**).

PRACTICAL: working, as in "can we have this bedside light **PRACTICAL**?" Also used to describe anything that actually works, like a stove, sink, radio.

PRODUCTION ASSISTANT: in film, the assistant to the producer; in television, the person responsible for logging all shots, timing them, and noting down all **TIME CODES**, as well as doing continuity notes—oh, and are sometimes asked to get the coffee as well. (No, I would never dare.)

PRODUCTION MANAGER: the coordinator of all business and technical matters; the person to whom directors plead for just a few more minutes, they are sure they will get the shot next time.

PULL FOCUS: (also **FOCUS PULL**; see **RACKING FOCUS**).

PULL-BACK: to move the camera away.

PUSH-IN: move the camera in closer. Especially in a multicamera studio, for example, "Camera 3 **PUSH-IN** to the announcer." It is sometimes also used to get the camera to **ZOOM** in a bit.

Q: (see **CUE**).

RACKING FOCUS (also **PULL FOCUS**): changing the focus from foreground to background, or vice versa—much loved by trendy directors (me too!).

RADIO MIKE: small microphone hidden about you, that picks up your voice and transmits it by radio via a bulky lump hidden in your clothing. Picks up all thumps and noises, often goes wrong, and fatal to keep wearing when going about your daily business not on the set. (Yes, we can still hear you.)

REACTION SHOT: the shot of what one actor is doing or "thinking," while the other is speaking.

REVERSES: shooting the opposite direction of what we have just done. After shooting all the shots of the person speaking to you, we will now do all your **REVERSES**.

ROLL TAPE: What you say to start off a video recording. If using single camera video, you flatter your cameraperson if you use the film term of **TURN OVER** instead, for then we can all pretend we are making major movies, rather than nice domestic dramas.

ROSTRUM CAMERA: a fixed camera that shoots static shots of books, pictures and so on, that will be slotted into a documentary or news program.

ROUGH CUT: the first rough putting together of a sequence or complete show. It is often used as much to work out what to cut to get the program onto time, as it is to see how effective it all is going to be.

RUNNING: what the camera operator says when the camera is ready and stabilized to start shooting.

RUNNING ORDER: the actual order in which the scenes will be recorded.

RUNNING TIME: the length of a program.

RUSHES: (see **DAILIES**).

SCANNER: the mobile control room used for video cameras.

SCRIPT GIRL: (see **CONTINUITY GIRL**).

SECAM: (Sequential Color And Memory) the color system used by France, and sold by them to Russia, so they now have to use it as well.

SETUP: the camera's position; a certain number of **SETUPS** are expected each day, depending on the scale of the production.

SHOOTING RATIO: the amount of film shot compared with the amount that will be in the final production. Film dramas have a **SHOOTING RATIO** of 1:10; film documentaries of 1:30; and video dramas of about 1:5.

SHOOTING SCRIPT: the final approved script, often with cameras and cutting points marked in.

SHOT ABBREVIATIONS: (see **ECU**; **CU**; **MCU**; **MS**; **WS**; **LS**; **ELS**; **BG**; **FG**; **POV**; **OTS**).

SHOTS: the pictures taken by the camera.

SIGHT LINE: the line of vision someone takes; a **SIGHT LINE** from one actor to another; from an audience member to the screen, or to a person on a stage.

SINGLE (also **ONE-SHOT**): shot of one person, usually in a medium close-up.

SINGLE CAMERA VIDEO: a technique for making programs using only a single camera (as in film) but recording the results on videotape.

SLATE: (see **CLAPSTICK BOARD**).

SOFT: out of focus. To prevent this is why the camera crew will ask you to stand in the different places you will be for a sequence for them to mark down your focus points.

SPARKS: Electricians, also known as **JUICERS**.

SPECIAL EFFECTS: anything that is achieved by tricks such as miniatures, computer generated images, split screens, etc.

SPEED: what the camera operator calls out when the camera is ready for the take. The sound operator can also call this out when the recorder is stabilized.

STAND IN: a double or near likeness of a main performer who literally stands in for him as a shot is lined up. This allows the tedium of finding out how to light scenes, and marking up where the performers should stand to be at the expense of those who are paid less. (It also allows the star to concentrate all his talent on the performance, and not waste it on working out the mechanics.)

STEADICAM: trade name for the device of harness and springs that allows a camera person wearing it to run after the performers and have the camera steady, more or less. (Well, it is sometimes also referred to as Wobblycam by those who prefer the macho of **HAND HELD.**)

STORY LINE: the brief synopsis of a film or production; the ongoing stories (as opposed to scripts) as planned for a soap drama.

STORYBOARD: a cartoon-like layout of all the shots planned and how they relate to each other, so everyone concerned (director, producer, designer, lighting, sound) can anticipate problems and plan for them. Some major movies like *Gone With the Wind* had all the **STORYBOARDS** drawn and colored before the director got onto the job.

STRIKE (see also **KILL**): remove or take away; "**STRIKE** the furniture"; "**STRIKE** that idea."

SWISH PAN (also **ZIP PAN**; **WHIP PAN**): a very quick swing of the camera, leaving the background as a blur. Often used to join two similar sequences together, one swish pan melding into the next one.

SWITCHER (also **VISION MIXER**): the person in the studio who switches between the video cameras, choosing which one's output is to be broadcast (live shows) or recorded.

TAKE: the individual shot, that is often repeated. Don't despair until the number gets above 50.

TELECINE: The machine in the television complex that allows film to be shown on television, and so any program made on film can easily be transmitted on any television system (such as **NTSC**, **PAL**, or **SECAM** for example). This is what goes wrong when they can't show a film clip in the middle of the news, and look embarrassed instead.

TELEPHOTO: a very long lens that makes distant people look as if they are near. It also makes them look as if they are walking fast but getting nowhere.

TELEPROMPTER (also **AUTOCUE**): trade name for the device in the studio that has the script rolling across the camera lens as far as the reader is concerned, so you at home are amazed they can speak so well without referring to their notes or script.

THREE-SHOT: three people in frame (**3-S**).

TIC: Tongue in cheek (ironic), usage limited to a small area of Liverpool.

TIGHT: close; the opposite of loose.

TILT UP/DOWN: the camera **TILTING UP** to look up, **TILTING DOWN** to look down; the correct term for **PAN** up/down.

TIME CODE: the electronic signal put onto the videotape so we all know exactly what was recorded where (that is, as long as someone remembered to write down the **TIME CODE** for the individual bits or takes).

TRACKING: (see **DOLLYING**).

TRACKS: the actual rails put down for the **DOLLY** to travel along.

TREATMENT: halfway between a **STORY LINE** and a **SHOOTING SCRIPT**. An indication of how the production will be, without all the dialogue.

TRUCKING: (see **DOLLYING**).

TURN OVER: Always used to start off a film camera (and often a video one as well—see **ROLL TAPE**).

TWO-SHOT (also **DOUBLE**): two people in the frame (**2-S**).

UPSTAGE: farther away from camera. This is a term taken from the theater, where in the old days the stages were on a slant, so being **UPSTAGE** was being farther from the audience. (An actor **UPSTAGING** you is one farther away, and so not seen by you, who is doing stuff that the audience will watch rather than you.)

VISION MIXER: (see **SWITCHER**).

VOICE-OVER [**VO**]: the disembodied voice that speaks whilst pictures are shown; the voice exhorting you to buy the product, or narrating the documentary. It is adored by actors who like to be paid without having to memorize lines.

VCR: video cassette recorder/recording.

VTR: video tape recorder/recording.

WHIP PAN: (see **SWISH PAN**).

WIDE ANGLE: the camera "sees" a broad view.

WILD TRACK: the sounds and effects recorded after the actors have said their lines, sometimes just of background (**ATMOS**), sometimes of the business that the actors have done. "Can we just **WILD TRACK** you walking upstairs with no dialogue?"

WIPE FRAME: a person or object going across the screen, often used to motivate a cut.

WRAP: the end, either of a day's shooting, or of the whole project. "It's a **WRAP**" is encouraging if you have worked hard all day, discouraging if you are still trying to get just one last shot into the camera.

WS: wide shot.

ZIP PAN: (see **SWISH PAN**).

ZOOM: changing the field of view by using an adjustable lens; also describes the actual adjustable lens that allows the camera to **ZOOM** in and out, or when very fast to **CRASH ZOOM**. Since it is something we cannot do with our own eyes, it tends to bring attention to the mechanics of the shot. Modern directors often **ZOOM** instead of moving the camera (and purists say "What a mistake!").

INDEX